Schizophrenia

About the Authors

Steven Silverstein, PhD, is Director of Schizophrenia Research at the University of Medicine and Dentistry of New Jersey's University Behavioral HealthCare and Robert Wood Johnson Medical School. He is currently Chair-Elect of the American Psychological Association's Committee for the Advancement of Professional Practice (CAPP) Task Force on Serious Mental Illness and Serious Emotional Disturbance.

William Spaulding, PhD, is Professor of Psychology at the University of Nebraska-Lincoln, and Chair of the CAPP Task Force on Serious Mental Illness.

Anthony Menditto, PhD, is Director of Treatment Programs at Fulton State Hospital and Clinical Associate Professor, Department of Psychiatry and Neurology, University of Missouri School of Medicine.

Advances in Psychotherapy – Evidence-Based Practice

Danny Wedding; PhD, Prof., MPH, St. Louis, MO
(Series Editor)
Larry Beutler; PhD, Prof., Palo Alto, CA
Kenneth E. Freedland; PhD, Prof., St. Louis, MO
Linda C. Sobell; PhD, Prof., ABPP, Ft. Lauderdale, FL
David A. Wolfe; PhD, Prof., Toronto
(Associate Editors)

The basic objective of this new series is to provide therapists with practical, evidence-based treatment guidance for the most common disorders seen in clinical practice – and to do so in a "reader-friendly" manner. Each book in the series is both a compact "how-to-do" reference on a particular disorder for use by professional clinicians in their daily work, as well as an ideal educational resource for students and for practice-oriented Continuing Education. The Society of Clinical Psychology is planning a system of home study CE accreditation based on the series.
The most important feature of the books is that they are practical and "reader-friendly": All are structured similarly and all provide a compact and easy-to-follow guide to all aspects that are relevant in real-life practice. Tables, boxed clinical "pearls," marginal notes, and summary boxes assist orientation, while checklists provide tools for use in daily practice.

Schizophrenia

Steven M. Silverstein, William D. Spaulding,
and Anthony A. Menditto

Library of Congress Cataloguing-in-Publication Data

is available via the Library of Congress Marc Database under the
LC Control Number 2006926587

Library and Archives Canada Cataloguing in Publication

Silverstein, Steven M.
Schizophrenia / Steven M. Silverstein, William D. Spaulding and Anthony A. Menditto.

(Advances in psychotherapy—evidence-based practice)
Includes bibliographical references.
ISBN 0-88937-315-9

1. Schizophrenia—Treatment. 2. Schizophrenia. I. Spaulding, William D. (William Delbert),
1950– II. Menditto, Anthony A. III. Title. IV. Series.

RC514.S544 2006   616.89'806   C2006-902537-1

© 2006 by Hogrefe & Huber Publishers

Cover art by Irene Kleinman

PUBLISHING OFFICES

USA:	Hogrefe & Huber Publishers, 875 Massachusetts Avenue, 7th Floor, Cambridge, MA 02139, Tel. (866) 823-4726, Fax (617) 354-6875, E-mail info@hhpub.com
EUROPE:	Hogrefe & Huber Publishers, Rohnsweg 25, 37085 Göttingen, Germany, Tel. +49 551 49609-0, Fax +49 551 49609-88, E-mail hhpub@hogrefe.de

SALES AND DISTRIBUTION

USA:	Hogrefe & Huber Publishers, Customer Service Department, 30 Amberwood Parkway, Ashland, OH 44805, Tel. (800) 228-3749, Fax (419) 281-6883, E-mail custserv@hhpub.com
EUROPE:	Hogrefe & Huber Publishers, Rohnsweg 25, 37085 Göttingen, Germany, Tel. +49 551 49609-0, Fax +49 551 49609-88, E-mail hhpub@hogrefe.de

OTHER OFFICES

CANADA:	Hogrefe & Huber Publishers, 1543 Bayview Avenue, Toronto, Ontario, M4G 3B5
SWITZERLAND:	Hogrefe & Huber Publishers, Länggass-Strasse 76, CH-3000 Bern 9

Hogrefe & Huber Publishers
Incorporated and registered in the State of Washington, USA, and in Göttingen, Lower Saxony,
Germany

Printed and bound in the USA
ISBN 0-88937-315-9

Preface

The intent of this book is to provide an overview of current conceptualizations of, and treatments for, schizophrenia. The focus of the book is on psychological treatments for the disorder as these interventions are relatively ignored in graduate and medical training about schizophrenia, even though the evidence for their effectiveness is comparable to that of pharmacologic treatment, with the combination of the two typically producing the best treatment outcomes.

There are several challenges when writing a book about schizophrenia. One is that the definition of the disorder is still being debated (e.g., is it best conceptualized as a disease or a syndrome? does it represent one or many conditions? what phenomena are most closely associated with it?). Another challenge is that in the current zeitgeist, schizophrenia is typically described as a brain disorder, with the implication that it represents an unfolding of a genetic or otherwise biologically determined pattern. Recent evidence, however, suggests the possibility that brain dysfunction in schizophrenia can result from the damaging effects of chronic environmental stress, such as that associated with childhood abuse, social defeat, drug use, and immigration. As a result of the continuing uncertainties about the validity of the construct of schizophrenia, and new evidence about its etiology, our position throughout this book is that: (1) despite what is known, much more remains to be known about the nature and causes of schizophrenia before it can be accurately viewed as a disease; and (2) the available evidence implies that schizophrenia is best not conceptualized narrowly as a disorder of brain physiology and treated in all cases with pharmacotherapy. A popular analogy today is that taking neuroleptic medication for schizophrenia is equivalent to taking insulin in cases of diabetes. In our view, this is both oversimplistic and incorrect. Rather, people diagnosed with schizophrenia have a complex condition, typically involving abnormal brain activity, overreactivity to environmental stress, and multiple cognitive and skills deficits that serve to promote abnormal coping and learning experiences. As such, psychological treatments are essential to restore healthy cognitive and social functioning, and to achieve maximal community integration. This book reviews psychological interventions that have demonstrated the greatest promise toward fulfilling this goal.

We hope this book is useful to a wide range of people, from students first learning about schizophrenia, to advanced clinicians and researchers who are looking for a review of current treatments and conceptualizations of the condition. Our goal is for this book to contribute to an ongoing dialog about what schizophrenia is and how it should best be treated. It is our hope that this book may motivate readers to approach the evidence on schizophrenia with an open mind, and thereby spark an interest in making further contributions to the current scientific debate and treatment development efforts.

Acknowledgments

The authors would like to thank Danny Wedding for providing the opportunity to write this book, and for his guidance during the writing process. Steve Silverstein would like to thank his mentors and teachers who taught him about schizophrenia and its treatment, including Ray Knight, Michael Raulin, Frank Miller, Jim Bowman, Robert Liberman, Chuck Wallace, and Rich Hunter. He would also like to thank his parents and Lindsay for their love and support; and Cotton for his continued inspiration. Will Spaulding would like to thank Rue Cromwell and Gordon Paul for guiding his early work in schizophrenia, and Mary Sullivan for ongoing love, support, and teamwork. Anthony Menditto thanks Gordon Paul for his pioneering work that laid the groundwork for applying rigorous standards of practice to developing services and properly evaluating them for individuals with severe mental disorders, and for the personal support and guidance he has provided to each of us over the years. He would also like to thank Lynn Geeson and Theresa Menditto for their love and support. We also thank Sarah Berten for her thorough and excellent editing and for her help maintaining the reference section through several edits of the manuscript.

Table of Contents

1

Description

1.1 Terminology

Schizophrenia is a diagnostic term describing a serious mental disorder that affects approximately 1% of the population worldwide, with a current global prevalence calculated at over 20 million people. It is typically diagnosed in late adolescence or early adulthood, and can be associated with lifelong disability, especially when appropriate services are not provided. It has been estimated that as many as ten percent of all disabled persons in the United States are diagnosed with schizophrenia (Rupp & Keith, 1993). The diagnosis accounts for 75% of all mental health expenditures and approximately 40% of all Medicaid reimbursements (Martin & Miller, 1998). Among people with the diagnosis, only between 10% and 30% are employed at any one time (Attkisson et al., 1992), and few of these people are able to maintain consistent employment (Policy Study Associates, 1989). Studies have consistently found that quality of life among people diagnosed with schizophrenia is significantly poorer than among the rest of the population (Lehman, Ward, & Linn, 1982). The economic costs of treating people diagnosed with schizophrenia have been estimated to be 62.7 billion dollars (e.g., including direct treatment costs and lost business productivity due to patient and family caretaker work absence) (Wu et al., 2005).

Despite advances in psychopharmacology, new medications do not work better than older ones (Lieberman et al., 2005), many patients have suboptimal responses, and relapse rates remain high (Kane & Marder, 1993). The most likely reason for the latter is that medications do not and can not address the social disability and skills deficits that many people diagnosed with schizophrenia have, due to the social and cognitive consequences of having a psychotic disorder, and to premorbid developmental abnormalities. These deficits in living skills are thought to be major factors involved in the high stress levels and impoverished support systems of many patients, and in their high vulnerability to relapse (Liberman & Corrigan, 1993). It is generally agreed, therefore, that, in addition to optimal medication treatment, schizophrenia patients require interventions that directly teach them the life skills needed to live successfully in the community. This statement is supported by research indicating that: (1) psychiatric symptoms are generally not strong predictors of treatment outcome or community functioning (Green, 1996), whereas the presence of specific skills deficits and cognitive deficits have been related to poorer outcomes across a number of domains (Green, 1996; Green, et al., 2000; Presly, Grubb, & Semple, 1982; Schretlen, et al., 2000; Silverstein, et al., 1998c); and (2) the likelihood of successful discharge from a hospital and adherence to an outpatient treatment program can be predicted by degree of social and adaptive living skills (Kopelowicz, Wallace, & Zarate, 1998; Paul & Lentz, 1977). Moreover, a meta-anal-

Medication does not address the social and instrumental skill impairments

ysis of 106 studies indicated that combined psychosocial and pharmacologic treatment demonstrated outcomes that were .39 standard deviations better than with medication alone, in addition to relapse rates that were 20% lower over a twelve month period (Mojtabi, Nicholson, & Carpenter, 1998).

Outcomes from treatment that include psychosocial interventions are better than those from medication alone

In this book, we will review currently available psychological assessment and treatment methods for treating people diagnosed with schizophrenia, and provide suggestions for future development in these areas. First, however, we introduce several concepts necessary for a basic understanding of the way schizophrenia is conceptualized and treated today.

1.1.1 Schizophrenia

Eugen Bleuler saw schizophrenia as a family of related disorders

The modern concept of "schizophrenia" has its origins in the work of Emil Kraepelin, who used the term *dementia praecox*, "early dementia." In the early 20th century the Swiss psychiatrist Eugen Bleuler introduced the term "schizophrenia" as he extensively modified the concepts underlying Kraepelin's "dementia praecox." "Dementia" is inappropriate, Bleuler argued, because many people appear to recover in ways inconsistent with an irreversible progressive brain disease. Bleuler also argued that the extensive individual differences between people in the diagnostic group suggest that there is not a single disorder, but a "family" of similar but distinct disorders. He argued that the most important characteristic of the disorder is not its onset, but the particular nature of its expression in the domain of human functioning we recognize today as *cognition*. He therefore proposed "schizophrenia," derived from Greek for "severed mind," to suggest the the fragmentation of mental functioning, as well as the split between thinking and feeling. Ambiguous translation of the Greek "schiz" led to the unfortunate and totally erroneous association of schizophrenia with "split personality" in popular culture.

It is important to note that "schizophrenia" cannot technically be considered a specific disease in that it has no known cause, and has varying clinical presentations and outcomes. The criteria for diagnosis are based largely on symptoms that, traditionally, have been most obvious in clinical practice, even though these can be highly variable across people, and over time and across psychotic episodes in the same person. Features that appear to be more specific to the condition, and to phases of the disorder, such as cognitive and psychophysiological abnormalities, have not yet been accepted by the American Psychiatric Association or World Health Organization (WHO) into official diagnostic criteria. "Schizophrenia" may be a "family" of disorders as Bleuler suggested, or a collection of disorders that have nothing in common other than the symptoms that comprise the diagnostic criteria. There is no pattern of symptoms unique to schizophrenia. In terms familiar to psychologists, "schizophrenia" does not have construct validity. Social policy discussions and even treatment approaches increasingly use the more inclusive term *serious mental illness* (SMI), which tends to be more informative and meaningful than "schizophrenia" or related specific diagnoses. In this book, "schizophrenia" is used in reference to specific findings based on subjects who meet the diagnostic criteria, and "serious mental illness" (SMI) is used when findings are probably generalizable to a broader population of individuals.

1.1.2 Positive, Negative, and Disorganized Symptoms

Symptoms characteristic of schizophrenia are often categorized into one of these three categories. Positive symptoms refer to those that represent an abnormal experience added onto what is normal (e.g., hearing voices that are not there; unusual beliefs). Negative symptoms refer to those that represent an absence of a normal experience (e.g., a reduced ability to experience pleasure, reduced motivation, blunted affect). Disorganized symptoms refer to a fragmentation of experience or behavior (e.g., formal thought disorder, purposeless motor activity). In schizophrenia, the concept of negative symptoms is sometimes subdivided into primary and secondary negative symptoms. Primary negative symptoms are considered those that directly reflect a disease process, whereas secondary symptoms are those that are due to side effects of medication (e.g., sedation) or other factors. A persistent clinical presentation involving primary negative symptoms has been termed the deficit syndrome, and there is evidence that this is a distinct subtype of schizophrenia (Kirkpatrick et al., 2001). The positive-negative symptom typology is based on the work of the 19th century British neurologist John Hughlings-Jackson, and his conceptualization of symptoms in neurologic disorders such as epilepsy. An alternative means of conceptualizing the symptoms of schizophrenia, one rooted in phenomenology, and in which these symptoms are not seen solely as additions to or deletions from normal functioning, is provided by Sass and Parnas (2003). Beck and Rector (2005) provide a view of symptoms that is rooted in cognitive theory.

1.1.3 Medical Model

As typically used, *medical model* refers to a combination of presumptions, including that: (1) schizophrenia is a monolithic biological disease; (2) the symptoms of schizophrenia are the most important targets of treatment; (3) *pharmacotherapy* (drug treatment) is the primary, if not sole treatment for schizophrenia; and (4) psychiatrists are or should be the primary practitioners, directors, and supervisors of all treatment.

1.1.4 Psychiatric Rehabilitation

Psychiatric rehabilitation refers to a treatment approach that typically combines many of the assessments and interventions described later in this book. The goal of psychiatric rehabilitation programs is to directly improve psychosocial functioning. The paradigm underlying psychiatric rehabilitation is different from that of the traditional medical model. While the medical model focuses on the identification of signs and symptoms of illness and their removal through medical intervention, rehabilitation focuses on the reduction of disability and the promotion of more effective adaptation in the individual's environment by using specific interventions to improve coping and behavioral abilities. Psychiatric rehabilitation is based on the assumption that adequate community adaptation is a function of three factors: the characteristics of the individual (e.g., symptoms, cognitive abilities, personality, etc.), the community's requirements for adequate functioning, and the supportiveness of the environment (Wallace, Li-

The goal of psychiatric rehabilitation is to reduce disability

berman, Kopelowicz, & Yaeger, 2000). Therefore, each of these three domains is a focus of assessment and treatment. In the past 25 years, the field of psychiatric rehabilitation has developed and expanded greatly, and much is now known about the application of this approach to schizophrenia (Corrigan & Liberman, 1994; Heinssen, Liberman, & Kopelowicz, 2000; Liberman, 1992; Wallace et al., 2000). Reviews of this approach have consistently indicated that when assessments and interventions are individually tailored to patients' needs, and comprehensive services are provided, significant improvement in functioning can occur (Liberman et al., 2005).

1.1.5 Recovery

Recovery is central to psychiatric rehabilitation, where it refers to the process of overcoming disabilities, but its meaning extends beyond that. Recovery is also closely associated with a social movement of the late 20th century in which people diagnosed with schizophrenia, in their roles as consumers of mental health services, organized to promote mental health reform. In that context, the concept has acquired connotations of hope for a better future as well as overcoming the effects of schizophrenia. As a result, the meanings of recovery are quite diverse, and considerable cross-fertilization and hybridization of the concept is going on between the scientific and consumer communities. Nevertheless, current usage always includes the ideas of overcoming disability and treatment goals being defined with or by the consumer, and most usage strongly connotes a rejection of "medical model" services.

Researchers see recovery as remission of symptoms, whereas people with schizophrenia as a process of reestablishing meaning in their lives

The two main classes of definitions of *recovery* involve the distinction between outcome and process. Recovery as an outcome has considerable overlap with the concept of remission. That is, a person who is recovered is seen as a person whose symptoms and disabilities are either no longer present, or are reduced to the point of not interfering significantly with daily living. Defined in this way, recovery can be operationalized readily, facilitating studies of groups of individuals. In contrast, recovery as a process implies that the perspective of the recovering person is one of rediscovering meaning in life apart from the effects of the mental illness. There is no implication here that this needs to occur within the context of a relationship with a psychiatric treatment provider. When such a relationship does exist, however, the ideal is that the provider and consumer share a common focus on helping the client achieve meaningful involvement in client-defined life areas. That is, treatment is not solely focused on clinician-defined goals, which typically involve (for people diagnosed with schizophrenia) reduction in symptoms and side effects.

1.1.6 Evidence-Based Practice

This term refers to a recent movement within the professional and scientific healthcare communities. It reflects the idea that clinical practice should be based upon and informed by scientific research. While this may seem like a platitude, especially in the clinical psychology community where calls for science-based clinical practice have been ubiquitous for over 50 years, there is a surprising degree of controversy about exactly how evidence-based practice should work. The idea can also be subsumed under the broader rubric of *best practices*, which incorporate social values and economic considerations as well as data from experimental research. For present purposes, evidence-based practice is a specific subdomain of best practices, wherein scientific support for specific clinical methods is the primary value.

1.2   Definition

Schizophrenia is diagnosed by confirming the presence of typical signs and symptoms, by ruling out other potential causes of these phenomena, and by noting the presence of disability and reduction in functioning over time. There is no single sign or symptom that is characteristic of all schizophrenia patients. Disorders that can present with similar symptoms to schizophrenia are reviewed below. Diagnostic criteria are covered in this section.

Currently, there are two sets of diagnostic criteria by which schizophrenia may be diagnosed. One is the American Psychiatric Associations *Diagnostic and Statistical Manual of Mental Dis*orders, 4th Edition, or as it is commonly referred to, DSM-IV (APA, 1994). The other system is the *International Classification of Diseases*, 10th Edition, or the ICD-10. Criteria sets from each system are presented in table form below, beginning with DSM-IV.

Table 1
DSM-IV Diagnostic Criteria for Schizophrenia (American Psychiatric Association, 1994)

Characteristic symptoms:

A. Two (or more) of the following, each present for a significant portion of time during a 1-month period (or less if successfully treated):

1) delusions

2) hallucinations

3) disorganized speech (e.g., frequent derailment or incoherence)

4) grossly disorganized or catatonic behavior

5) negative symptoms, i.e., affective flattening, alogia, or avolition

B. *Social/occupational dysfunction:* For a significant portion of the time since the onset of the disturbance, one or more major areas of functioning such as work, interpersonal relations, or self-care are markedly below the level achieved prior to the onset (or when then onset is in childhood or adolescence, failure to achieve expected level of interpersonal, academic, or occupational achievement).

C. *Duration:* Continuous signs of the disturbance persist for at least 6 months. This 6-month period must include at least 1 month of symptoms (or less if successfully treated) that meet Criterion A (i.e., active-phase symptoms) and may include periods of prodromal or residual symptoms. During these prodromal or residual periods, the signs of the disturbance may be manifested by only negative symptoms or two or more symptoms listed in Criterion A present in an attenuated form (e.g., odd beliefs, unusual perceptual experiences).

Table 1
continued

D. *Schizoaffective and Mood Disorder exclusion*: Schizoaffective Disorder and Mood Disorder with Psychotic Features have been ruled out because either (1) no Major Depressive, Manic, or Mixed Episodes have occurred concurrently with the active-phase symptoms; or (2) if mood episodes have occurred during active-phase symptoms, their total duration has been brief relative to the duration of the active and residual periods.

E. *Substance/general medical condition exclusion*: The disturbance is not due to the direct physiological effects of a substance (e.g., a drug of abuse, a medication) or a general medical condition.

F. *Relationship to a Pervasive Developmental Disorder*: If there is a history of Autistic Disorder or another Pervasive Developmental Disorder, the additional diagnosis of Schizophrenia is made only if prominent delusions or hallucinations are also present for at least a month (or less if successfully treated).

Classification of longitudinal course (can be applied only after at least 1 year has elapsed since the initial onset of active-phase symptoms):

- Episodic with Interepisode Residual Symptoms (episodes are defined by the re-emergence of prominent psychotic symptoms); *also specify if*:
- With Prominent Negative Symptoms
- Episodic with No Interepisode Residual Symptoms
- Continuous (prominent psychotic symptoms are present throughout the period of observations); *also specify if*: With Prominent Negative Symptoms
- Single Episode in Partial Remission; *also specify if*: With Prominent Negative Symptoms
- Single Episode in Full Remission
- Other or Unspecified Pattern

Note: Only one Criterion A symptom is required if delusions are bizarre or hallucinations consist of a voice keeping up a running commentary on the person's behavior or thoughts, or two or more voices conversing with each other.

Table 2
ICD-10 Diagnostic Criteria for Schizophrenia (World Health Organization, 1992)

Definition

The schizophrenic disorders are characterized in general by fundamental and characteristic distortions of thinking and perception, and by inappropriate or blunted affect. Clear consciousness and intellectual capacity are usually maintained, although certain cognitive deficits may evolve in the course of time. The disturbance involves the most basic functions that give the normal person a feeling of individuality, uniqueness, and self-direction. The most intimate thoughts, feelings, and acts are often felt to be known to or shared by others, and explanatory delusions may develop, to the effect that natural or supernatural forces are at work to influence the afflicted individual's thoughts and actions in ways that are often bizarre. The individual may see himself or herself as the pivot of all that happens. Hallucinations, especially auditory, are common and may comment on the individual's behavior or thoughts. Perception is frequently disturbed in other ways: colors or sounds may seem unduly vivid or altered in quality, and irrelevant features of ordinary things may appear more important than the whole object or situation. Perplexity is also common early on and frequently leads to a belief that everyday situations possess a special, usually sinister, meaning intended uniquely for the individual. In the characteristic schizophrenic disturbance of thinking, peripheral and irrelevant features of a total concept, which are inhibited in normal directed mental activity, are brought to the fore and utilized in place of those that are relevant and appropriate to the situation. Thus thinking becomes vague, elliptical, and obscure, and its expression in speech sometimes incomprehensible. Breaks and interpolations in the train of thought are frequent, and thoughts may seem to be withdrawn by some outside agency. Mood is characteristically shallow, capricious, or incongruous. Ambivalence and disturbance of volition may appear as inertia, negativism, or stupor. Catatonia may be present. The onset may be acute, with seriously disturbed behavior, or insidious, with a gradual development of odd ideas and conduct. The course of the disorder shows equally great variation and is by no means inevitably chronic or deteriorating (the course is specified by five-character categories). In a proportion of cases, which may vary in different cultures and populations, the outcome is complete, or nearly complete, recovery. The sexes are approximately equally affected but the onset tends to be later in women.

Although no strictly pathognomonic symptoms can be identified, for practical purposes it is useful to divide the above symptoms into groups that have special importance for the diagnosis and often occur together, such as:

a) thought echo, thought insertion or withdrawal, and thought broadcasting;

b) delusions of control, influence, or passivity, clearly referred to body or limb movements or specific thoughts, actions, or sensations; delusional perception;

c) hallucinatory voices giving a running commentary on the patient's behavior, or discussing the patient among themselves, or other types of hallucinatory voices coming from some part of the body;

d) persistent delusions of other kinds that are culturally inappropriate and completely impossible, such as religious or political identity, or superhuman powers and abilities (e.g.,being able to control the weather, or being in communication with aliens from another world);

e) persistent hallucinations in any modality, when accompanied either by fleeting or half-formed delusions without clear affective content, or by persistent overvalued ideas, or when occurring every day for weeks or months on end;

f) breaks or interpolations in the train of thought, resulting in incoherence or irrelevant speech, or neologisms;

g) catatonic behavior, such as excitement, posturing, or waxy flexibility, negativism, mutism, and stupor;

h) "negative" symptoms such as marked apathy, paucity of speech, and blunting or incongruity of emotional responses, usually resulting in social withdrawal and lowering of social performance; it must be clear that these are not due to depression or to neuroleptic medication;

i) a significant and consistent change in the overall quality of some aspects of personal behavior, manifest as loss of interest, aimlessness, idleness, a self-absorbed attitude, and social withdrawal.

Diagnostic Guidelines

The normal requirement for a diagnosis of schizophrenia is that a minimum of one very clear symptom (and usually two or more if less clear-cut) belonging to any one of the groups listed as (a) to (d) above, or symptoms from at least two of the groups referred to as (e) to (h), should have been clearly present for most of the time during a period of 1 month or more. Conditions meeting such symptomatic requirements

Table 2
continued

but of duration less than 1 month (whether treated or not) should be diagnosed in the first instance as acute schizophrenia-like psychotic disorder and are classified as schizophrenia if the symptoms persist for longer periods.

Viewed retrospectively, it may be clear that a prodromal phase in which symptoms and behavior, such as loss of interest in work, social activities, and personal appearance and hygiene, together with generalized anxiety and mild degrees of depression and preoccupation, preceded the onset of psychotic symptoms by weeks or even months. Because of the difficulty in timing onset, the 1-month duration criterion applies only to the specific symptoms listed above and not to any prodromal nonpsychotic phase.

The diagnosis of schizophrenia should not be made in the presence of extensive depressive or manic symptoms unless it is clear that schizophrenic symptoms antedated the affective disturbance. If both schizophrenic and affective symptoms develop together and are evenly balanced, the diagnosis of schizoaffective disorder should be made, even if the schizophrenic symptoms by themselves would have justified the diagnosis of schizophrenia. Schizophrenia should not be diagnosed in the presence of overt brain disease or during states of drug intoxication or withdrawal.

1.3   Epidemiology

The prevalence rate of schizophrenia is approximately the same in all cultures

The extent of disability varies considerably across cultures

The prevalence of schizophrenia in the general population is generally found to be about 1–1.5%. That is, about 1–1.5% of all people meet the DSM or ICD diagnostic criteria for schizophrenia at some point in their lives. The diagnosis is most commonly made in late adolescence or early adulthood. Cross-cultural studies suggest the 1–1.5% rate is fairly consistent across cultures. However, there may be differences in *morbidity*, the degree to which the illness causes disability or other impairments. People in more industrial cultures who meet diagnostic criteria for schizophrenia may suffer more severe disabilities than those in less industrial cultures.

Epidemiological findings have been influential in the evolution of the view that schizophrenia is among other things a *neurodevelopmental* disorder. Patterns of relationships between the incidence of schizophrenia and factors such as birth complications, neurological soft signs (abnormalities that do not denote specific neurological disease), minor physical anomalies (e.g.,malformation of capillaries in the nailbed), season of birth (e.g., the second trimester of gestation occurs during a cold season) and environmental stress during gestation (droughts, famines, invasion) all suggest that developmental compromise of the CNS is often an etiological factor. The stable cross-cultural incidence rate is also cited as evidence of a common underlying biological etiology.

1.4   Course and Prognosis

1.4.1   Short-Term Outcomes

Data on the early, short-term course of schizophrenia are typically portrayed as negative. However, many negative outcomes are the result of noncompliance with treatment or comorbid substance abuse. For example, Gitlin et al. (2001) demonstrated that among young schizophrenia patients who discontinued their medication, over 70% of patients relapsed in the first year, and over 90% by two years. Other data have demonstrated that using drugs or alcohol nearly doubles the rate of relapse over 1–2 years in schizophrenia (Maslin, 2003).

Short-term outcomes can be positive when people collaborate with treatment providers

When adequate treatment is provided, however, data on short-term recovery are often more positive. For example, in a study of first-episode patients with schizophrenia who were enrolled into a standardized treatment (medication) algorithm study, 74% of patients achieved full symptom remission within one year (Loebel et al., 1992). Similarly, at a specialized clinic for young people with psychosis in Melbourne, Australia, 91% of young people with recent onset of psychosis were in relatively complete remission of symptoms after one year of assertive community treatment (ACT), medication, and cognitive behavior therapy (CBT) (Edwards et al., 1998). In a study at the UCLA Aftercare Clinic, 80% of people with recent onset schizophrenia who stayed in treatment achieved remission of symptoms within their first year of treatment (Gitlin et al., 2001). In a similar study from Nova Scotia, 83% of people recovering from a first-episode of schizophrenia were not rehospitalized within the first year, and more than half of the 83% were involved in full or part time work or education (Whitehorn et al., 2004). These data on positive outcomes with optimal treatment echo older findings indicating that low- or intermittent-dosing strategies increase the risk of relapse severalfold (e.g., Herz et al., 1991).

Using drugs or alcohol doubles the risk for relapse in schizophrenia

1.4.2   Long-Term Outcomes

Paul and Lentz (1977) demonstrated that even patients considered treatment-refractory could benefit from treatment when this consisted of intensive social-learning based inpatient services followed by declining contact aftercare. In that study, long-stay hospital patients who were treated in the social learning program achieved a 97% discharge rate (compared to a 50% rate in traditional, custodial care), 1200% improvement in adaptive, social, cognitive, and instrumental outcomes (compared to negligible improvements with other treatment models), and only an 11% rate of needing antipsychotic medication at discharge, compared to 100% of patients in the custodial care condition.

Other demonstrations of positive long-term outcomes followed-up patients many years after being in the hospital. For example, Huber et al. (1975), followed-up 502 people after an average period of 22 years. In this study, 26% of the sample had achieved full recovery in both psychological and social functioning. Another 31% demonstrated significant improvement. These data led the authors to conclude that "Schizophrenia does not seem to be a disease of slow progressive deterioration. Even in the second and third decades of illness, there is still potential for full or partial recovery" (Huber et al. 1980). Similar results were found in M. Bleuler's (1978) follow-up study of 208 people with schizophrenia. In the Iowa 500 study (Tsuang et al., 1979), 186 patients were followed-up an average of 35 years later. In this sample, 20% were considered recovered, an additional 26% considered considerably improved, 21% were married, 12% were divorced, and 35% were employed.

Ciompi (1980) conducted a 37-year follow-up study and reported that 20.1% of patients were completely recovered, 42.6% were improved, 29.8% were unchanged, 5.9% were functioning more poorly than at the initial assessment, and the fate of 1.6% of the patients was uncertain. Harding et al. (1987) followed-up a cohort of 269 patients who had been treated on the back wards of a state psychiatric hospital in Vermont in the 1950s. The follow-up period was 20–25 years and all subjects were rediagnosed according to DSM-III criteria. For half to 2/3 of subjects who meet DSM-III criteria for schizophrenia ($N = 82$), long-term outcome was characterized by an evolution into various degrees of productivity, social involvement, wellness, and competent functioning; 68% of subjects displayed no signs or symptoms of schizophrenia at follow-up and 45% displayed no psychiatric symptoms at all. A follow-up study compared these subjects to matched patients from Maine. In the 1950s, whereas Vermont developed comprehensive community-based rehabilitation programming that was linked to state hospital census reduction, Maine did not, instead relying on medication and hospital based aftercare services, with little in the way of rehabilitation. In this study (DeSisto et al., 1995a, 1995b), during the follow-up period, Vermont subjects worked more, had fewer symptoms, and had better community adjustment and global functioning than Maine subjects.

Long-term outcomes in schizophrenia can be positive when people have access to appropriate services

WHO sponsored a major study (Sartorius et al., 1977) which examined incidence, course, and prognosis of schizophrenia in various developed and developing countries. Studies examining two and five-year follow-up outcomes from this sample indicated that among people in developing countries, over 60% were asymptomatic or functioning well, compared to less than 20% in developed countries. In a later replication using the same design (Jablensky et al., 1992), similar results were found. These data indicate that the course of schizophrenia is heavily influenced by the environment in which the patient lives.

1.5   Differential Diagnosis

Because there is no single feature that is common to all cases of schizophrenia, and no test that can confirm the diagnosis, diagnosis of the disorder must be made by exclusion. This is made more difficult by the multitude of other conditions that can present with similar symptoms. In the tables below, other disorders that need to be taken into account when making a differential diagnosis of schizophrenia are listed.

When the conditions listed in these tables can be confidently ruled out, and the patient meets criteria for schizophrenia defined by DSM-IV or ICD-10, a diagnosis of schizophrenia is appropriate. Note that a patient presenting with an initial psychotic episode can be very difficult to diagnose, due to the duration criterion that differentiates schizophrenia from some other psychotic disorders. That is, a patient with the requisite symptoms should be given a diagnosis of

Table 3
General Medical Conditions That Can Produce Psychotic Symptoms

Nutritional Deficiency Syndromes	Infectious Diseases
Pellegra	Cerebral cysts and abscesses
Pernicious anemia	Cerebral malaria
Vitamin A deficiency	Encephalitis caused by herpes simplex
Vitamin D deficiency	Encephalitis due to other causes
Magnesium deficiency	HIV encephalopathy
Selenium deficiency	Prion diseases (e.g., Creutzfeldt-Jacob)
Zinc deficiency	Lyme disease
	Neurosyphilis
Endocrine Disorders	Rheumatic endocarditis
Addison's Disease	
Cushing's syndrome	**Autoimmune Diseases**
Hyperparathyroidism	Addison's disease
Hyperthyroidism	Multiple sclerosis
Hypoparathyroidism	Rheumatic fever/chorea
Hypopituarism	Scleroderma
Hypothyroidism	Systemic lupus erythematosus
Metabolic Diseases	**Chromosomal Abnormalities**
Adrenoleukodystrophy	Fragile X syndrome (females)
Adrenomyeloneuropathy	Noonan syndrome
Fabry's disease	Velo-cardio-facial syndrome
GM$_2$ gangliosidosis	Turner syndrome
Hartnup disease	Kleinfelter syndrome
Wilson's disease	XXX karyotype
Homocystrinuria from MTHFR deficiency	XYY karyotype
Metachromatic leukodystrophy	
Porphry	

Other CNS Diseases	
Cerebrovascular lesions	Hydrocephalus of late onset
Cranial trauma	Kartagener's syndrome
Pick's disease (and other dementias)	Intracranial tumors
Dentatorubral-pallidoluysian atrophy	Marchiafava-Bignami disease
Epilepsies	Oculocutaneous albinism
Familial basal ganglia calcification	Sarcoidosis
Friedrich's ataxia	Schilder's cerebral sclerosis
Huntington's disease	Tuberous sclerosis
Uremia	

Note. Based on H.A. Nasrallah & D.J. Smeltzer (2003). *Contemporary diagnosis and management of the patient with schizophrenia.* Newtown, PA: Handbooks in Health Care.

Table 4
Substances That Can Produce Psychotic Symptoms

Drugs of Abuse: During Intoxication
Alcohol
Amphetamine (including methamphetamine, methylphenidate, other sympatho-mimetics)
Cannabis (marijuana, hashish, sensimilla, THC)
Cocaine
Hallucinogens (including LSD, mescaline, peyote, and MDMA or "ecstasy")
Volatile inhalants (e.g., gasoline, glue, paint thinner)
Opiods
PCP and other NMDA receptor blockers (e.g., ketamine, cyclohexamine)
Sedatives, hypnotics, and anxiolytics (e.g., barbiturates, benzodiazepines, and carbamates)

Drugs of Abuse: During Withdrawal
Alcohol
Sedatives, hypnotics and anxiolytics

Therapeutic Drugs
Antibiotics (e.g., procaine penicillin, cephalosporins)
Anticholinergic agents (e.g., atropine, benztropine)
Anticonvulsants (e.g., phenytoin, ethosuximide)
Antidepressants
Antihypertensive agents (e.g., methyldopa, hydralazine)
Antimalarial agents
Antituberculosis agents
Antiviral agents (e.g., acyclovir, interferon)
Appetite suppressants (e.g., diethylpropion, phenteramine)
Benzodiazepines and similar hypnotics
Cardioactive drugs (e.g., digitalis, procainamide)
Dopaminergic agents (e.g., levodopa, amantadine, bromocriptine)
Endocrine agents (e.g., corticosteroids, thyroid hormones, clomiphene)
Nonsteroidal anti-inflammatory agents (e.g., sulindac, indomethacin, ibuprofen)
Psychostimulants and sympathomimetics
Pulmonary agents (e.g., albuterol, ephedrine, pseudoephedrine)
Other therapeutic drugs (e.g., asparaginase, baclofen, cimetidine, cyclosporine, disulfiram, methysurgide, pentazocine)

Toxins
Arsenic
Bismuth
Bromine
Carbon monoxide
Copper
Magnesium
Manganese
Mercury
Thallium

Note. Based on H.A. Nasrallah & D.J. Smeltzer (2003). *Contemporary diagnosis and management of the patient with schizophrenia.* Newtown, PA: Handbooks in Health Care.

Table 5
Other Psychiatric Disorders That Can Present With Psychotic Symptoms
Psychotic Disorders
Brief psychotic disorder (distinguished from schizophrenia by illness duration criterion)
Schizophreniform disorder (distinguished from schizophrenia by illness duration criterion)
Delusional disorder
Schizoaffective disorder
Shared psychotic disorder (folie à deux)
Psychotic disorder not otherwise specified
Mood Disorders
Major depression
Bipolar disorder
Personality Disorders
Borderline personality disorder
Schizotypal personality disorder
Dissociative Disorders
Multiple personality disorder (especially hallucinations)
Other Disorders
Posttraumatic stress disorder (especially hallucinations)
Pervasive developmental disorders (especially disorganized thinking)

schizophreniform disorder if the duration of the condition appears to be shorter than 6 months. After 6 months, however, the diagnosis would be changed to schizophrenia. It is also often not possible to differentiate between schizophrenia and bipolar disorder with psychotic features during the initial psychotic episode. This is because both can present with the same psychotic symptoms, and, as discussed in the section on comorbidity, agitation and mood symptoms are common during acute psychotic episodes in people with schizophrenia. In such cases, information about response to treatment and subsequent clinical course are used to eventually make a definitive diagnosis.

1.6   Comorbid Conditions

People diagnosed with schizophrenia often have other psychiatric and medical difficulties in addition to psychotic symptoms. In this section, we will review the psychiatric conditions and issues which are frequently found and that need to be targets of treatment. Following this, we discuss medical issues that are often found among schizophrenia patients.

20–50% of people with schizophrenia attempt suicide; about 10% die by suicide

1.6.1   Psychiatric Conditions

Depression and Suicide

Depression is commonly comorbid with schizophrenia, especially among patients with an awareness that what is happening to them is part of a disorder. Lifetime estimates of major depression in people diagnosed with schizophrenia typically range from 25–33% of patients, with some studies reporting rates as high as 80%. Estimates of the rate of schizophrenia patients who meet criteria for a depressive syndrome at a single point in time have been reported to be as high as 10% among inpatients and 50% among outpatients (Kirkpatrick & Tek, 2005).

Suicide is a major problem in schizophrenia. Estimates of the lifetime frequency of suicide attempts among people with the disorder range from 20–50%, and multiple studies have reported that close to 10% of people diagnosed with schizophrenia kill themselves. While suicide in schizophrenia may have multiple causes, including command hallucinations, depression is generally recognized as the major precipitating factor.

Substance Abuse

People diagnosed with schizophrenia have been reported to abuse tobacco, alcohol, and street drugs more than people in the general population (McCreadie, 2002). Estimates of smoking have been as high as 90% of patients in some studies. Various theories have been proposed to account for this high rate of tobacco use, including that it reduces side effects by lowering blood levels of antipsychotic medication by as much as 50%, and that it improves cognitive functioning by stimulating the nicotinic form of cholinergic receptor, where abnormalities have been found to exist in patients.

Multiple studies and reviews suggest that the rate of other drug use approximates 50% in people with schizophrenia. Surprisingly, hallucinogenic drugs such as LSD are commonly used, in addition to marijuana and cocaine. The use of street drugs in people diagnosed with schizophrenia is a critical treatment target because these drugs can increase the rates of psychotic symptoms, leading to relapse and rehospitalization. The same is true with alcohol use, which studies show can be found in as many as 40% of schizophrenia patients (lifetime), with rates close to 20% at any one time (Kirkpatrick & Tek, 2005).

Repetitive Behaviors

Polydipsia, a condition involving excessive water intake, is frequently found among hospitalized patients, with rates reported as high as 25% in some studies. This is a dangerous condition because it can lead to electrolyte imbalances, and therefore to other problems such mental status changes ("water intoxication"), cardiac arrhythmias, and even death. Other repetitive behaviors that may be found among severely ill patients include pica, bulimia, and hoarding of objects.

Obsessive-Compulsive Symptoms

Obsessive-compulsive symptoms are found among schizophrenia patients to a higher degree than in the general population, with estimates ranging from 15–25%, and estimates for a diagnoses of obsessive-compulsive disorder only slightly lower (Tibbo & Warneke, 1999). The presence of obsessive-compulsive symptomatology in schizophrenia is usually a poor prognostic indicator. Comorbidity of schizophrenia with obsessive-compulsive symptoms may reflect disordered brain functioning involving the basal ganglia.

Anxiety Symptoms and Disorders
Recent studies suggest that anxiety is a significant clinical problem in many patients diagnosed with schizophrenia, both during the initial psychotic episode and over the long term. Anxiety problems can occur as generalized anxiety or as discrete panic attacks. In some cases anxiety may be appear to clinically independent of psychotic symptoms, whereas in other cases it may be appear to be a result of hearing command hallucinations or of past experiences of psychosis (e.g., a form of PTSD caused by experiencing psychotic symptoms).

Learning Disabilities
The lifetime prevalence of schizophrenia in the learning disabled population has been estimated to be 3%–12% (Heaton-Ward, 1977; Parson et al., 1984). This is significantly higher than the rate of schizophrenia in the general population, which has been consistently estimated at approximately 1%. Patients diagnosed with both disorders, compared to patients with only schizophrenia, have been found to have higher rates of negative symptoms, episodic memory deficits, soft neurological signs, and epilepsy, and to receive more community supports (Doody et al., 1998). Structural MRI data indicate that the brains of people with both disorders resemble those of people with schizophrenia alone (Sanderson et al., 1999). The comorbidity of learning disability with schizophrenia is not thought to be an artifact of the cognitive deficits typically associated with schizophrenia, but rather, to be due to a preexisting learning disability that may characterize a subset of schizophrenia patients (Condray, 2005). In support of the hypothesis of common mechanisms involved in both disorders, data indicate that learning disability (dyslexia) is associated with abnormalities in the magnocellular pathway (Vidyasagar, 2001), and with integration of information (Simmers & Bex, 2001), which are the mechanisms that have been proposed to account for backward masking and perceptual organization deficits in schizophrenia (Keri et al., 2005; Silverstein et al., 2000; see also Silverstein & Palumbo, 1995 for a discussion of similarities between schizophrenia and some forms of nonverbal learning disabilities).

1.6.2   Medical Conditions

People with schizophrenia die from natural causes at approximately 1.5 times the expected rate. This is thought to be due to the poor health care that they receive, secondary to multiple factors including living in poorer neighborhoods, reduced access to health care, reduced initiative in seeking healthcare, poorer nutrition, and effects of tobacco, alcohol and drug abuse. One condition specifically related to smoking that has been found to be elevated in schizophrenia is chronic obstructive pulmonary disease (COPD). A second that appears to be related to drug use, or impaired decision making secondary to drug use, is an increased prevalence of HIV infection.

Certain medical conditions may emerge as the result of taking second-generation antipsychotic medications. Many patients experience significant weight gain when taking these medications (e.g., an average gain of 30 lbs from olanzapine). This obesity can then cause other medical problems, such as sleep apnea, cardiovascular problems, and diabetes. While some cases of diabetes may be a direct result of the medication itself, it is generally accepted that many cases are secondary to weight gain. Medical complications that can result from first-generation antipsychotic medications include tardive dyskinesia (involuntary muscle activity, often involving the tongue or face), dystonic reactions, muscle rigidity, and akithesia (a subjective sense of restlessness, often associated with pacing). In the 1970s and 1980s, the strategy of initiating medication with high doses (i.e., "rapid neuroleptization") led to many cases of neuroleptic malignant sydrome (NMS), which is a life-threatening condition with a high death rate. NMS is characterized by fever, muscular rigidity, altered mental status, and autonomic dysfunction.

1.7   Diagnostic Procedures and Documentation

There is no single test that can be used to diagnose schizophrenia. As noted above, psychotic symptoms can be found in other psychiatric and general medical disorders. A diagnosis of schizophrenia is made by ruling out other causes of psychotic symptoms, behavioral disturbance, and functional disability, and by ensuring that a patient meets DSM-IV criteria for the disorder. Still, schizophrenia is a heterogeneous disorder and even patients in the same phase of the disorder (see below, section on treatment planning) can present with markedly different symptoms, maladaptive behaviors, and levels of functional impairment. In clinical practice, what is most important is to document the nature and severity of the symptoms and disability, to systematically assess the extent of change in response to treatment over time, and then modify the treatment accordingly in a hypothesis-driven fashion. In the section on assessment (Section 3.1) below, a number of instruments for rating symptoms, cognitive dysfunction, behavior dysfunction, and functional impairment are discussed, with an emphasis on those that are now considered state-of-the-art. Despite the existence of these measures, they are rarely used on a regular basis outside of clinical research contexts. Regular assessment and discussion of findings with patients, however, can form the basis of the collaborative approach that is at the heart of recovery-oriented care.

2

Theories and Models of Schizophrenia

The etiology of schizophrenia is still not known. However, a number of phenomena have been consistently associated with the disorder, and several leading theories are based around these findings. Today, theories which posit biological factors as primary causes are currently widely accepted. However, recent evidence indicates that psychological neglect and trauma, and other environmental factors are strongly associated with the development of schizophrenia. Therefore, what is needed are sophisticated theories that can account for both suspected primary biological causes (e.g., genetic factors), as well as environmental factors that can alter brain development and function and gene expression. Ultimately, any comprehensive theory of the disorder will need to integrate psychological and biological factors and their interactions in explaining the signs, symptoms and disabilities associated with schizophrenia. Below, leading theories of the etiology of schizophrenia will be highlighted.

2.1   Genetics

It is now clear that having a parent with schizophrenia raises a child's risk of having the disorder from 1% to approximately 10%. Having an identical twin with schizophrenia increases the risk factor to approximately 50%. Data also indicate an increase in rates of schizotypal personality disorder in families that include a person with schizophrenia. These data suggest that schizophrenia is likely to be caused by multiple genes, and that when some, but not all, of these are inherited, less severe forms of the illness are demonstrated. To date, eight chromosomal sites have been associated with an increased risk for schizophrenia.

A different view of the role of genes in schizophrenia has been proposed by Tienari, Wynne, and colleagues (Tienari et al., 2004). In this view, the genes responsible for schizophrenia lead to a greater than normal plasticity in the developing brain. This view comes from data examining the interaction of genetic risk for schizophrenia with the type of home environment in which adopted-away children of mothers with schizophrenia were raised. Data from the longitudinal Finnish Adoption Study indicate that at-risk children reared in homes with chaotic environments with high stress levels and poor communication developed schizophrenia at a higher rate than other people at-risk. However, at-risk children raised in "enriched" homes with good communication skills developed schizophrenia at a lower than normal rate, and many of these children were particularly talented in one or more areas. The data from the Finnish Adoption Study are consistent with earlier theorizing by Bender (1966) about the excessive degree of cortical plasticity among children with schizophrenia.

Leading theories of the biological causes involve genetic, viral, birth complication, neuroanatomical, neurophysiological, and neurodevelopmental evidence

If one identical twin has schizophrenia, the risk of the other twin developing it is approximately 50%

2.2   Theories Involving Viral or Immunopathology

Viral and immune system-related theories of schizophrenia remain popular, despite the lack of strong and consistent evidence for any of them. Currently, there are six theories being actively researched (Buchanan & Carpenter, 2005). One involves retroviral infection, which is a type of virus that becomes part of the person's genome and alters gene expression (and that of offspring). Evidence for retroviral activity has been found in postmortem studies, although active evidence of activity has not been found in live patients. A second theory involves active viral infection of the brain. It is known that viruses that attack the brain can cause mental status changes, either immediately, or delayed over many years. However, evidence for viral infection has not been found consistently in schizophrenia patients. A related theory holds that the infection occurs very early in life, creating brain changes that represent a vulnerability to development of schizophrenia, even if the virus is no longer present later in life. This theory fits with other neurodevelopmental models of schizophrenia, but is not supported by much evidence at this point. The viral theory with perhaps the strongest evidence involves maternal exposure to viral infection during pregnancy. Specifically, several studies indicate increased rates of schizophrenia among offspring of mothers exposed to or treated for influenza infections during their second trimester of pregnancy (e.g., Mednick et al., 1994). Two final viral theories involve immune system functioning. One version involves abnormal immune reactions to viruses, leading to alterations in brain tissue and function that cause psychopathology. A second version involves a virus causing an autoimmune disorder, where the immune system begins to destroy the body's own tissue. A similar, but nonviral theory states that schizophrenia is a form of autoimmune disorder involving the brain.

2.3   Birth Complications

There is greater evidence that birth complications play a role in the development of schizophrenia. Studies, differing in methodology, have indicated that three types of difficulties are related to an increased rate of developing the disorder: pregnancy complications (e.g., bleeding, Rh incompatibility), delivery complications (e.g., hypoxia), and/or abnormal fetal development (e.g., low birth weight, reduced head size) (Buchanan & Carpenter, 2005). It is less clear what the causes of these problems are; the extent to which they are caused by genetic and/or abnormal developmental factors is unknown.

2.4   Neuroanatomy

Earlier theories localizing schizophrenia symptoms to single brain structures have been replaced by those that focus on interactions between regions. The regions most implicated in such theories are the frontal lobes, the temporal lobes, and the basal ganglia. Recent work also suggests that the cerebellum,

thalamus, and hippocampus play significant roles. There is evidence supporting each of these views. For example, decreased prefrontal inhibition of lim-
bic system circuitry can account for the emergence of phenomena such as
hallucinations. Hypofrontality can also account for negative symptoms. Theories focusing on the disturbed integration of mental activity focus on alterations in thalamic activity. Similarly, an alteration in cerebellar functioning
could account for faulty temporal signalling, which may also be involved in
reduced integration of information. Andreasen et al. (1998) posited that schizophrenia involves a disturbance in a pathway, and in feedback loops, involving the cortex, thalamus, and cerebellum. This theory can account for a range
of symptoms and cognitive deficits in schizophrenia, although it lacks specificity and has not been rigorously tested. The hippocampus has been implicated in developmental theories of schizophrenia (Walker & DiForio, 1997).
Specifically, increased stress initiates a set of reactions leading to an increase
in cortisol, which, if occurring on a chronic basis, can damage the hippocampus. Hippocampal damage has been implicated in a variety of psychotic phenomena, including decontextualizing of memories (which may be involved
in experiencing memory traces as hallucinations), and alterations of self-ex-
perience (Read et al., 2001, 2005; Danion et al., 1999), both of which are
common in schizophrenia (Sass, 1992).

> **Reduced functioning of NMDA receptors could lead to less modulation of sensory input by memory and other contextual influences**

A recent view posits that schizophrenia involves a fundamental disturbance
in neuronal connectivity and communication (i.e., "cognitive coordination")
that is found throughout the cortex (Phillips & Silverstein, 2003). One possible
cause of this is hypofunction of NMDA receptors, which are involved in mod-
ifying neural integration based on prior experience. However, reductions in cognitive coordination could also be caused by factors such as excessive neuronal
pruning in adolescence. The theory that schizophrenia involves a widespread
disturbance in cognitive coordination and its underlying neural basis is supported by findings of multiple forms of reduced stimulus organization (e.g., in visual
and auditory perceptual organization, memory organization, and thought and
speech organization), and significant correlations between these disturbances
(reviewed in Uhlhaas & Silverstein, 2005).

2.5 Neurophysiology

The most influential neurophysiological theory of schizophrenia is that of the
dopamine hypothesis. This theory grew out of several lines of evidence, including: (1) the emergence of psychotic symptoms in people who abused ampheta-
mines, cocaine, and other drugs which are known to increase brain dopamine;
(2) emergence of psychotic symptoms in Parkinson's disease patients who receive excessive doses of L-dopa, a dopamine precursor; and (3) the positive
effects of antipsychotic medication in controlling positive symptoms, and the
known ability of these medications to block dopamine receptors in vitro. Despite this consistent evidence, however, the theory has not received strong support from studies examining dopamine metabolites in the spinal fluid of patients, or from postmortem studies, although this may be due to significant
methodological difficulties in conducting such studies.

People who later develop schizophrenia often have neuromotor abnormalities in infancy and early childhood

More recent theories of schizophrenia implicate hypofunction of the NMDA type of glutamate receptor, which is involved in mediating experience-dependent adaptation (Javitt & Zukin, 1991; Olney & Farber, 1995) and connectivity between pyramidal cells, and altered GABAergic activity. While glutamate is the primary excitatory neurotransmitter in the brain, GABA is important for inhibitory activity between interneurons, which act on pyramidal cells to further promote experience-dependent adaptation. Alterations in NMDA and GABA are thought to underlie the widespread cognitive coordination disturbances in schizophrenia that were noted above (Phillips & Silverstein, 2003).

Another neurotransmitter implicated in schizophrenia is serotonin. In the 1950s and 1960s, research studies and clinical observations on the emergence of psychotic symptoms following administration of LSD, mescaline, and other drugs known to increase serotonergic activity suggested a link between serotonin and schizophrenia. However, some medications known to increase psychotic symptoms in schizophrenia (e.g., clozapine), actually work by increasing brain serotonin.

Rather than trying to isolate a single neurotransmitter system, it is increasingly recognized that interactions among neurotransmitter systems may be important for understanding schizophrenia. For example, administration of phencyclidine (PCP) or ketamine leads to blockade of NMDA receptors but also to increases in prefrontal dopamine turnover, both of which are associated with schizophrenia. New developments in the psychopharmacology of schizophrenia also involve a focus on multiple neurotransmitter systems. Thus, whereas first-generation antipsychotic medications (e.g., haloperidol, chlorpromazine) were chosen for their ability to block dopamine receptors, new drug development often target multiple systems, including dopamine, glutamate, serotonin, and norepinephrine (see Section 4.2 on Mechanisms of Action).

2.6   Neurodevelopment

Neurodevelopmental theories view schizophrenia as involving abnormalities throughout the lifespan, with varying expressions of neuropathology during different phases of development. Direct evidence for a neurodevelopmental view of schizophrenia comes from the work of Fish (1987) and Walker (1994). In a series of studies, Fish and colleagues have identified a number of developmental abnormalities in high-risk children, which, collectively, they called pandysmaturation. Similarly, Walker and colleagues have identified abnormal motor and postural activity in children who later developed schizophrenia. This, along with evidence that positive symptoms diminish later in life while motor abnormalities increase, led to the hypothesis that schizophrenia manifests itself in the brain regions that are most metabolically active at a given stage in development.

2.7   Environmental Factors

Recent research indicates that several forms of environmental stress and/or trauma may be involved in increasing the likelihood that schizophrenia will develop. One body of evidence suggests that neglect and trauma during child-hood increase the risk for developing the disorder later in life. These data include findings that childhood abuse is associated with increased rates of adult schizophrenia, and that high rates of neglect and physical and sexual abuse are found in the histories of people with schizophrenia (Read & Argyle, 1999; Read et al., 2005). Increased severity of abuse is also related to poorer premorbid functioning and to decreased cognitive functioning in selected do-mains among schizophrenia patients (Schenkel et al., 2005). Read et al. (2005) suggest that the stress caused by abuse can lead to hippocampal dam-age, which can then lead to decontextualization of the memories of the abuse experiences, resulting in the experience of hallucinations. This, plus other CNS changes can thereby constitute an environmentally-mediated biological diathesis for the disorder.

Urban birth, urban upbringing, and migration to urban areas within a person's country of origin are also strongly related to an increased risk for schizophrenia (Pedersen et al., 2001). These findings cannot be accounted for by increased drug use, or by a tendency for mentally ill people to converge on urban areas. An intriguing possibility is that the effect of urban environments on schizophre-nia is mediated by exposure to a virus. While the data on this hypothesis are not strong, some evidence suggests that viral exposure (e.g., to Toxoplasmosis gon-dii) may increase risk (Yolken et al., 2001).

An additional environmental factor related to schizophrenia is international migration. A number of studies and a recent meta-analysis and review (Cantor-Grae & Selten, 2005) provide strong evidence that migration to a new country is associated with increased risk for schizophrenia. The findings were strongest for people migrating from developing countries to developed countries, and for people of black skin color. Among migrating populations, rates of schizophrenia are significantly higher than among the native populations of the countries from which people migrated. Moreover, there is a lower incidence of schizophrenia when nonwhite ethnic minorities live in areas where minorities make up a larger than normal (for that country) proportion of the local population. This evidence suggests that these data are not due to a selection bias wherein people who are more likely to migrate are more prone to schizophrenia.

Cantor-Graae and Selten (2005) suggest that the long-term experience of social defeat and stress associated with being an underprivileged minority, or outsider, may be a causative mechanism in schizophrenia (see also van Os et al., 1996). Evidence for this comes from animal studies where social defeat leads to increased dopamine levels in areas such as the nucleus accumbens and prefrontal cortex, which are regions relevant to schizophrenia. While social de-feat is unlikely to be a sufficient cause of schizophrenia, it may interact with other factors to increase risk. As noted above, chronic stress can lead to ana-tomical changes in the hippocampus and other brain regions implicated in schiz-ophrenia. Thus, as with abuse, chronic severe stress may produce biological changes that, in combination with other psychological and biological factors, facilitate expression of the illness.

Environmental stress-ors (e.g., urban birth, sexual abuse) may lead to changes in brain functioning, pre-disposing someone to schizophrenia

2.8   Substance Abuse

In 1987, Andreasson et al. demonstrated a dose-response relationship between cannabis use and the later development of schizophrenia. Recently, there has been renewed interest in the possibility that cannabis use can actually precipitate the onset of schizophrenia – in addition to its use for self-medication in people who are experiencing symptoms. A recent meta-analysis of findings (Henquet et al., 2005) indicated that cannabis use more than doubles the risk of developing schizophrenia. These findings could not be explained by demographic factors, the presence of other drug use, or the presence of pre-existing symptoms that would imply self-medication rather than a causal role for cannabis. A recent study by Caspi et al. (2005) using data from a New Zealand birth cohort (Arseneault et al., 2002) demonstrated that cannabis interacts with the catechol-O-methyltransferase (COMT) gene to increase the risk for schizophrenia. Specifically, individuals homozygous for the COMT valine allele were most likely to exhibit psychotic symptoms and to develop schizophreniform disorder after adolescent exposure to cannabis. However, this relationship was not observed among cannabis users who had 2 copies of the COMT methionine allele. Moreover, cannabis use by itself was not associated with either COMT allele, indicating that the alleles are not related to increased use of cannabis. This type of interaction effect is important, as it brings together biological and behavioral theories of schizophrenia.

2.9   Cognitive Factors

Cognitive theories suggest that schizophrenia involves slowness of processing, reduced processing capacity, impaired selective attention, and reduced cognitive coordination and context processing abilities

The most influential current theories of cognitive impairment in schizophrenia attempt to account for multiple disturbances in cognition in terms of a single underlying impairment. For example, Carr and Wale (1986) noted that the perceptual organization problems in schizophrenia occurred in a variety of domains, including vision, audition, memory, thought, and motor activity. This led to the hypothesis that schizophrenia is characterized by a widespread disturbance in preattentive stimulus grouping. A similar hypothesis was put forward by Phillips and Silverstein (2003). They drew on work from neurobiology and computational theory as evidence that there is a fundamental cortical processing algorithm that is based on the ability to use contextual information to modify processing of stimuli (Phillips & Singer, 1997). This theory also drew on extensive evidence for stimulus organization deficits in schizophrenia and their relationships to thought disorder and conceptual disorganization, to posit an overall deficit in cognitive coordination, including both spatial and temporal processing. This view, which integrates cognitive findings with those of reduced lateral interactions between pyramidal cells in schizophrenia secondary to NMDA-receptor hypofunction (Javitt & Zukin, 1991), accounts for a number of cognitive, symptom, and social deficits found in the disorder.

Another view of context processing difficulties in schizophrenia was put forth by Cohen and Servan-Schreiber (1992). They focused on context processing as an aspect of working memory, and demonstrated that a single impairment could account for findings from multiple tasks on which schizophrenia patients perform poorly. The basis of this deficit was thought to be in reduced dopaminergic activity in the dorsolateral prefrontal cortex. Empirical studies using working memory tasks have supported the original theory (e.g., Cohen et al., 1999). While it was originally hypothesized that a context processing deficit would be associated with negative symptoms, studies demonstrate that it is most associated with disorganized symptoms (e.g., MacDonald et al., 2005), as predicted by the Phillips and Silverstein (2003) theory. This theory remains influential as a more specific account of the working memory (i.e., temporal processing) deficits found in schizophrenia patients. It cannot account, however, for the deficits in spatial context processing that have been consistently identified in the disorder (Uhlhaas & Silverstein, 2005).

In addition to theories which attempt to elucidate the core cognitive disturbance in schizophrenia, some researchers have focused on the interaction between cognitive deficits and stress in producing clinical deterioration. Green et al. (2000) discussed several potential models of the relationship between cognitive deficits and functional impairment in schizophrenia, based on a wealth of findings on specific cognitive predictors of outcome. Beck and Rector (2005) highlight the importance of distorted beliefs about the self and others in the development and maintenance of symptoms. The importance of these efforts is that cognitive deficits are now seen as core features of the disorder that affect multiple areas of functioning, and that are related to type and severity of disability. Therefore, understanding the types of cognitive deficits in schizophrenia, and their role in interacting with other aspects of the disorder, can both increase our understanding of the illness and help to develop more effective treatments.

3

Diagnosis and Treatment Indications

3.1 Assessment

3.1.1 Symptom Assessment

A comprehensive assessment of schizophrenia should always involve a thorough assessment of symptoms. Careful description of the frequency and intensity of symptoms can guide the choice of pharmacologic and behavioral methods targeted at symptom reduction (Haddock, et al., 1994; Schwarzkopf, Crilly, & Silverstein, 1999; Spaulding, et al., 1986). It is important to note, however, that symptom response is relatively independent of response to other targets of treatment (Carpenter, et al., 1976; Wallace et al., 2000). Thus, symptom assessment alone is insufficient as an assessment strategy for schizophrenia, where many other areas of potential disability (e.g., social and instrumental role functioning) will affect long-term prognosis.

> Critical domains for assessment are symptoms, cognition, and social and instrumental functioning

A number of symptom rating scales are currently in widespread use. These include the Brief Psychiatric Rating Scale (Ventura, et al., 1993); Scale for the Assessment of Negative Symptoms (SANS) (Andreasen, 1984a); Scale for the Assessment of Positive Symptoms (SAPS) (Andreasen, 1984b); and the Positive and Negative Syndrome Scale (PANSS) (Kay, Opler, & Fiszbein, 1987). Each of these provide important information on symptom dimensions and are based on theoretical models of symptomatology in schizophrenia. These measures are practically useful for detecting symptom change over time. However, they have a number of conceptual and methodological flaws which make their use problematic for research trying to understand symptom etiology (reviewed in Silverstein, 2000).

3.1.2 Functional Assessment

Recently, a number of instruments have been developed with the goal of providing the information needed for a comprehensive assessment of real-world functioning in a single measure. This is consistent with recent literature reviews and consensus conferences of stakeholders of mental health services that have developed criteria for functional assessment instruments (IAPSRS, 1997; Liberman, Kuehnel, & Backet, 1998; Menditto, et al., 1999; Smith, et al., 1997). Characteristics of these newer measures include: (1) the ability to assess, in both inpatient and outpatient settings, functioning in the types of roles characteristic of people with serious mental illnesses; (2) the inclusion of information from multiple sources; (3) a focus on strengths and skills rather than on deficits and symptoms; (4) assessment of a wide range of skills relevant for successful community living; (5) an easy to administer format; (6) established reliability and validity; and (7) an ease of translating the findings into a rehabilitation plan (Menditto et al., 1999).

One such new measure is the Client's Assessment of Strength, Interests, and Goals (CASIG; Wallace, et al., 2001). The CASIG is administered as a structured interview that begins by eliciting the individual's medium-term goals in five areas of community living; housing, money/work, interpersonal relationships, health, and spiritual activities. Follow-up questions clarify these domain-specific goals and ask the patient to specify to the best of their ability the services needed to achieve them. The rest of the CASIG involves questions assessing current and past community functioning, medication compliance and side effects, quality of life, quality of treatment, symptoms, and performance of intolerable community behaviors.

Another useful measure is the Independent Living Skills Inventory (ILSI) (Menditto et al., 1999). The ILSI was developed at the University of Nebraska to measure a person's ability to perform a range of skills needed for successful community living. A unique feature of the scale is that each item is rated along two dimensions. One is the degree to which the skill can be performed, and the other is the degree of assistance required to perform the skill. This scoring method is useful in planning a rehabilitation program because it distinguishes between skill deficits and performance deficits, each requiring different forms of intervention. The current form of the ILSI consists of eleven subscales, each representing a different domain of community functioning (e.g., money management, home maintenance, cooking, etc.). A similar but slightly older measure is the Independent Living Skills Survey (ILSS) (Vaccaro, Pitts, & Wallace, 1992). The ILSS consists of 188 items that assess performance in twelve areas of functioning. Both self-report and staff-rated versions of the ILSS are currently available. A recent study of the ILSS and ILSI demonstrated that they have excellent reliability and validity, and that they are sensitive to treatment effects (Menditto et al., 1999). In addition, both measures are relatively brief to administer, and have high face-validity making them relatively user-friendly.

One potential problem with self-report based measures of behavioral functioning is that patients with severe cognitive impairment, thought disorganization, and/or delusional thinking may provide inaccurate information. In general, self-report based measures such as the CASIG are most useful for outpatients, or for higher functioning inpatients and day hospital patients who are clearly able to articulate realistic goals and whose behavior approximates community standards. For other patients, where the treatment focus is on the elimination of inappropriate behaviors and the generation of independent living skills, performance-based and observational measures are the most appropriate. Multimodal behavioral assessment techniques (Barlow & Hersen, 1984; O'Brien & Haynes, 1993) can be useful in this regard. One class of behavioral assessment techniques involves role-plays (e.g., Bellack, et al., 1990; Bellack, et al., 1994), which have been found to provide important data that can guide treatment planning and gauge response to treatment. In addition to the self-report measures and rating scales described above, there are several comprehensive, observational assessment systems that have demonstrated utility for long-term inpatient treatment. A number of these were initially described in the landmark study of Paul and Lentz (1977) of inpatient social-learning-based treatment (see description of Social Learning Program below, in section on interventions). One of these measures is the Time Sample Behavioral Checklist (TSBC) (Paul, 1987), which is an observational rating scale used by staff to indicate the frequency of a range of appropriate and inappropriate behaviors. TSBC observations are made on a regular schedule during all waking hours for all patients in a residential treatment program, yielding a weekly average of about 100 observations per person. These observations allow a treatment team to track behaviors as specific as degree of social interactiveness, bizarre behavior, facial expression, and many others. A second measure developed by Paul and colleagues is the Clinical Frequencies Recording System (CFRS) (Paul & Lentz, 1977). This is also an observational scale, but it uses event-sampling procedures to record the occurrence of event-specific behaviors such as attendance and successful participation in groups as well as of low-frequency clinically critical behaviors (e.g., aggressive outbursts). The third key measure developed as part of the Paul and Lentz (1977) project is the Staff-Resident Interaction Chronograph (SRIC) (Paul, 1988). Data for the SRIC is recorded by noninteractive observers on the unit using stratified time-sampling techniques similar to those used with the TSBC. The purpose of the SRIC is to obtain data on the nature of staff-patient interactions. SRIC data can therefore be used to monitor adherence of staff to prescribed therapeutic behaviors as well as to evaluate entire treatment programs. The TSBC, CFRS, and SRIC have all demonstrated excellent psychometric characteristics, and have been successfully disseminated to treatment programs other than where they were developed. Together, these instruments can form the backbone of a residential treatment program.

Two functional measures which have been incorporated into the MATRICS (see below) secondary outcomes battery are the UCSD Performance-Based Skills Assessment (UPSA) (Patterson et al. 2001) and the Maryland Assessment of Social Competence (MASC) (Bellack et al. 2004). The UPSA assesses, via role-plays, skills in the following areas: household chores, communication, finance, transportation, and planning recreational activities. The MASC is a structured behavioral assessment that measures the ability to resolve interpersonal problems through conversation. On each administration, 4 scenarios are used, in 3-minute role-plays where a confederate plays different roles (e.g., employer, landlord, etc.). Alternate forms of the MASC are available (Bellack et al. 2004).

3.1.3 Cognitive Assessment

Cognitive assessment is important in schizophrenia, given the number of impairments associated with the disorder. Cognitive impairments are often found in the areas of visual information processing (Green, 1998; Knight & Silverstein, 1998); attention (Nuechterlein, 1991; Silverstein, Light, & Palumbo, 1998e); working memory (Docherty, et al., 1996; Park & Holzman, 1992; Silverstein et al., 1998a); short-term memory (Calev, et al., 1987; Silverstein, et al., 1998d); executive functioning (Goldberg, et al., 1987); context processing (Cohen, Barch, Carter, & Servan-Schreiber, 1999; Cohen & Servan–Schreiber, 1992; Silverstein, Matteson, & Knight, 1996); and social perception and cognition (Green et al., 2005; Silverstein, 1997). While no single profile of cognitive deficits has been found to characterize all schizophrenia patients, the majority have impaired ability in at least one area of functioning (Morice & Delehunty, 1996; Palmer et al., 1997).

Several short, but comprehensive test batteries are now available to assess cognition

A recent development in cognition research in schizophrenia involves the creation of standardized cognitive assessment batteries. Early versions of these represented compilations of available neuropsychological tests, combined to produce a relatively brief but sensitive assessment of cognition in schizophrenia. Examples of such batteries are the Repeatable Battery for the Neuropsychological Assessment of Schizophrenia (RBANS) (Gold et al., 1999; Hobart et al., 1999) and the Brief Assessment of Cognition in Schizophrenia (BACS) (Keefe et al., 2004).

A major initiative to standardized cognitive assessment is known as the Measurement and Treatment Research to Improve Cognition in Schizophrenia (MATRICS) project (Green et al., 2004). The MATRICS project involved the formation of several committees of established cognition researchers to reach consensus on which domains of cognition should be assessed and which tests should assess them. As of this writing, consensus has been reached, and kits to administer the MATRICS battery should be available by 2006.

A similar but larger project is based in Sydney, Australia under the name BrainNet (Williams et al., 2005). The purpose of the BrainNet initiative is to develop standardized, computer-based cognitive and psychophysiological assessment batteries (Paul et al., 2005), and to pool data from the world-wide use of these tools into a single international database. As of this writing, this database contains data from over 8,000 people, from age 6 on, and including various diagnostic groups, including schizophrenia, ADHD, Alzheimer's disease, depression, PTSD, and mild cognitive impairment (secondary to traumatic brain injury) (Gordon et al., 2005). The cognitive battery, called IntegNeuro, and the psychophysiological battery, called NeuroMarker, are currently being used in clinical trials and in clinical settings throughout the world, with all data collected being included in the international database.

Cognitive assessment should include both laboratory and self-report measures

A recently developed self-report measure of cognitive disability is the Subjective Scale to Investigate Cognition in Schizophrenia (SSTICS) (Stip et al., 2003). This 21-item, Likert-scaled, self-report measure inquires into several domains of cognition that are impaired in schizophrenia, including attention. Interestingly, SSTICS scores do not correlate highly with performance on laboratory tests of neuropsychological functioning (Prouteau et al., 2004), supporting arguments on the independence of *impairment* (i.e., poor performance on laboratory measures) and *disability* (i.e., reduced real-world functioning), and suggesting the need to assess both domains in the clinical assessment of schizophrenia.

3.1.4 Dynamic Assessment

Dynamic assessments measures performance under conditions of feedback and training

Most traditional cognitive and functional measures can be viewed as forms of static assessment in the sense that they measure the skills a person has at any given moment, as opposed to what they are capable of learning and therefore of a person's potential ability. This issue has been faced earlier in other areas, such as intelligence testing, and has led the development of methods of "dynamic assessment" or more specifically, "learning potential assessment" (Budoff, 1987). The goal of dynamic assessment is to quantify learning potential. This is accomplished by incorporating sensitive methods for assessing the ability to improve with instructions and/or practice into the testing conditions.

A face-valid form of dynamic assessment is called the Micro-Module Learning Test (MMLT) (Silverstein et al., 2005b). The MMLT, which has seven psychometrically equivalent alternate forms, is a brief measure of responsiveness to the three core components involved in skills training (see below): verbal instruction, modeling, and role play. The MMLT was developed, in part, because there was a need for a relatively brief and accurate assessment tool that would predict a patient's performance before being placed in a skills training intervention, which often lasts from three to six months. While successful prediction of performance in skills training has been achieved using traditional neuropsychological measures, an assumption driving the development of the MMLT was that by using the basic structure and content found in skills training procedures, greater ecological and predictive validity would be achieved. With the MMLT, clinicians can determine, before placing a patient in a skills training group, whether they are likely to benefit from that group, or whether they initially need other interventions, such as cognitive rehabilitation and/or attention shaping (see below).

3.2   Treatment Planning

Comprehensive treatment of people diagnosed with schizophrenia requires attention to three classes of factors: the phase of the disorder, the behavioral deficits and excesses that require intervention and treatments appropriate to address them, and a range of supportive services that can include supported education, supported housing, supported employment, financial support, case management, medical and dental care, and peer support (Liberman et al., 2005). By "phase of the disorder" we refer here to whether a person is in the prodromal phase of schizophrenia, the acute phase (usually requiring short-term hospitalization), the stabilizing phase (i.e., still with the presence of symptoms, but responding to treatment), the stable phase, in remission, or refractory to treatment. Each of these cases requires different types of care.

Treatment planning requires attention to the phase of the disorder, addressing behavioral strengths and deficits, and the recruitment of appropriate community supports

The discussion of treatment planning below is divided into two sections. The first covers inpatient treatment planning. Much of the focus of that section applies to treatment-refractory patients, where hospital stays are long enough to engage in an iterative process of assessment, treatment planning, initiation of interventions, assessment of treatment response, modification of the treatment plan, further assessment, etc. However, even in cases of acute psychosis, psychosocial interventions have been shown to be effective, including a token economy (LePage, 1999), cognitive behavior therapy (Drake & Bellack, 2005), cognitive rehabilitation (Medalia, Dorn, & Watras-Gans, 2000), and skills training to prepare people to return to the community (Smith et al., 1996). Community support services are not relevant to inpatient care per se, although they are critical to formulating a discharge plan for outpatient care.

3.2.1   Inpatient

For inpatient treatment planning, we recommend the use of the Multimodal Functional Model (MFM) developed by Hunter and colleagues (Wilkniss, Hunt-

The multimodal functional model is a data- and hypothesis-driven form of treatment planning

er, & Silverstein, 2004). The MFM reflects an integrative biomedical-psychological-socioenvironmental perspective on treatment planning. In addition to incorporating data collected using standard assessment tools, the MFM also makes use of specialized data collection instruments designed for residential settings. The ultimate goal of the approach is to design interventions to replace socially inappropriate adaptations with more normalized ones. The strength of this focus is that resulting interventions are no longer geared exclusively toward behavioral control and management but are *treatment* efforts that attempt to effect long-term change in the behaviors (or more specifically, the deficits and/or excesses) that led to psychiatric hospitalization.

3.2.2   MFM Diagnostic Formulations

Step 1: Assessing Triggering and Setting Conditions

First, the specific set of target symptoms and/or behaviors of concern are identified and operationally defined so all staff and the patient can readily recognize them when they occur and rate their intensity, duration and variability. Second, specific diagnostic formulations about the functional significance of the behaviors or symptoms are developed considering the larger context in which they occur. All staff should be involved in identifying current external (e.g., loss of loved one, few housing options) and internal (e.g., anxiety, chronic anger, iatrogenic sedation) stimulus conditions. Each stimulus condition is considered to serve either a primary or secondary instigating function. *Primary* influences (or "triggers") are those that must be present for the behavior (symptom) to occur. For example, a task demand in a harsh tone may set off an episode of aggressive behavior or an increase in hallucinations. *Secondary* instigating influences are "setting" conditions, or those whose presence increases or decreases the likelihood that a symptom or behavior will occur in the presence of the primary instigator. Examples include sleep deprivation, physical pain, extraneous uncontrollable noise, confusion, medication side effects etc. That is, the patient may not demonstrate the symptom in response to a demand in a harsh tone if he is not sleep deprived. Sleep deprivation sets him up for being more reactive to the harsh tone.

Step 2: Assessing the Function of the Behavior

Next, staff develop hypotheses about the purposes or functions being served by the behaviors/symptoms (e.g., modulating pain, avoiding rejection, seeking attention). It should be noted that some symptoms (e.g.,hallucinations) may more directly reflect underlying neurobiological abnormalities. However, even these symptoms often begin to acquire functional features as they become associated with distinct reinforcing consequences, and one can observe a change in frequency, duration or intensity related to specific consequences (e.g., getting attention, being left alone, etc.).

Step 3: Assessing Vulnerability Influences

Next, *tertiary*, or vulnerability, influences are assessed. Tertiary stimulus conditions are ongoing challenges or deficits that interact with primary and secondary stimuli that increase or decrease the probability of expression of the target behaviors or symptoms. Examples include sensory impairments, personality characteristics, and limited communication skills. These tertiary conditions serve as avenues for rehabilitation efforts and coping strategies that improve one's immunities to potential problems. Finally, attempting to model the interplay among primary, secondary, and tertiary stimulus conditions across both external and internal variables leads to a detailed understanding of how abnormal behaviors emerge and provides direction in the design of focused interventions.

Collecting Data

The diagnostic process should be a collaborative effort, and direct dialog with the patient concerning his/her perceptions of the significant influences on target behaviors (symptoms) along with his/her goals and motivations is crucial. In addition, collecting baseline data and continually collecting data during treatment are the second component to determining both instigating events and consequences as well as the dimensions of the behavior. Data collection tools used with the MFM include the Patterns and Trends Datasheet and CABC cards. The Patterns and Trends Datasheet is a record of the timing, frequency, duration and variability of the target behavior. It allows for collection of data every 1/2 hour of the day over a month's period so that patterns in the data may be easily discerned. The CABC cards allow for episodic collection of information on the context, antecedents, and consequences related to each event of the target behavior. When they are reviewed after several days, the factors influencing aggressive and violent behavior usually can be identified.

Functional Assessment and Analysis

For each symptom or behavior, the multidisciplinary team member most skilled in evaluation of a specific modality of influence will develop hypotheses about the instigating and exacerbating conditions specific to that modality purportedly related to the target behavior. Next, hypotheses about the level of influence of each condition (primary, secondary, tertiary) and the functional properties of the behavior are developed. Finally, ideas about possible interventions are formulated.

Linking Functional Diagnostic Hypotheses to Interventions

It is important to link each intervention to a specific hypothesis. For each hypothesis, a specific intervention or set of interventions is determined. The hypothesis is then tested via the intervention as part of a systematic staging plan that allows for testing one hypothesis at a time before introducing a new intervention. The expected change, based on objectively measurable goals, and a time frame within which that change should occur are recorded. Hypotheses, and related interventions which are deemed useful based on data are continued; those not useful after data collection and hypothesis testing are discarded and the next hypothesis is tested. As the system is deployed, there is an ever-increasing database about what works, how much each subsequent intervention adds to the treatment effect, and a record of what has previously been tried along with its effects. This system of case formulation and intervention results in a streamlined treatment program that over time include only those interventions that result in measurable benefits to the patient.

3.2.3 Outpatient

Comprehensive outpatient care typically requires the coordination of multiple services and agencies

Comprehensive outpatient care typically requires the coordination of multiple services and agencies. The services involved in outpatient care can include skills training, family intervention, supported employment, supported education, supported housing, individual and/or group psychotherapy, cognitive rehabilitation, integrated treatment for substance abuse and psychosis, assistance in accessing entitlements and appropriate medical and dental care, pharmacotherapy, and crisis assistance. Peer support also forms an important part of the recovery process for many people with schizophrenia, whether this be in the context of a psychosocial clubhouse or peer-run groups and services (such as Wellness Recovery Action Plan groups; see section on interventions below). Specific interventions are discussed in the next section.

4

Treatment

4.1 Methods of Treatment

4.1.1 Collaborative Psychopharmacotherapy

Combining psychiatric rehabilitation (see below) and pharmacotherapy is now considered standard practice, and evidence exists that this combination is more effective than medication alone (Mojtabai et al., 1998; Menditto et al., 1996). During the past fifteen years, significant advances have been made in our understanding of the interactions between these forms of treatment (Kopelowicz & Liberman, 1995). We now know, for example, that certain medications impair cognitive functions that are critical to rehabilitation success (Corrigan & Penn, 1995). This requires that the people prescribing medication, the rest of the treatment team, and the patient work together to reach a decision regarding a balance of residual symptoms and cognitive deficits that will maximize performance success in real-world roles at the current time. In addition, behavioral treatments have now successfully reduced positive symptoms such as hallucinations and delusions in both medication responders and nonresponders. This suggests that, among responders, medication dosages required to suppress these symptoms may be able to be lowered after behavioral treatment is initiated (Haddock, et al., 1994). Ongoing assessment is also required to determine if changes in cognition and/or symptoms over time require redesigning either the medication or psychosocial treatment strategy.

While combining pharmacotherapy and psychiatric rehabilitation is a generally accepted principle, it should be noted that the degree to which medication *must* be the cornerstone of treatment in *all* cases of schizophrenia remains unclear. For example, Paul and Lentz (1977) reported that many of their treatment refractory patients made substantial gains in their program, and were discharged with successful community tenure, even though they were not on medication. In addition, Mosher and colleagues (e.g., Mosher & Bola, 2000; Mosher & Menn, 1978) demonstrated that, in many cases, young patients undergoing their first or second psychotic episode can be successfully treated without medication in community residences with high staff-patient ratios that employ a treatment model based on existential psychological principles. In light of these generally ignored data, and because: (a) medication noncompliance rates in schizophrenia can reach up to 75% (Kissling, 1992; Lieberman et al., 2005), and (b) side effects (e.g., weight gain, sedation, etc.) are complicating factors (and a cause of noncompliance), treatment providers need to continually and empirically determine the lowest amount of medication that is required in any individual case. Just as importantly, it behooves clinicians to make the fullest use of psychosocial interventions, given their demonstrated effectiveness. Along these lines,

Comprehensive treatment planning must balance symptom reduction from medication with ability to engage in psychological treatment and function in life roles

For many patients, increased alertness and better role functioning is achieved with lower medication doses even if this means some persistence of symptoms

more research is needed into the degree of medication necessary to achieve good outcomes within the context of an optimal psychosocial treatment matrix. Nearly all studies of medication effectiveness have been conducted without the benefit of the full arsenal of effective psychiatric rehabilitation interventions. Thus, we still really do not know the impact that rehabilitation interventions can have relative to pharmacotherapy in treating people with schizophrenia.

4.1.2   Rehabilitation Counseling

Rehabilitation counseling is driven by the client's goals and is consistent with recovery-oriented care

Rehabilitation counseling, primarily associated with the work of William Anthony and his colleagues (Anthony, Cohen, & Farkas, 1990) represents a fusion of key concepts and principles from traditional physical rehabilitation and traditional client-centered psychotherapy. Rehabilitation counseling typically involves a periodic meeting between the person in recovery and at least one other member of the treatment and rehabilitation team. Both directive and nondirective psychotherapy techniques are employed to identify the problems that require treatment and rehabilitation, the person's desires and concerns, and resources to be applied. The initial objective is to reach consensus about the person's needs and what the team can do about them. A subsequent objective is to construct an individualized treatment and rehabilitation plan that integrates the team's goals and objectives with specific interventions and other services, bearing in mind that the person in recovery and/or substitute decision makers are key members of the team. All the pharmacological and psychosocial modalities to be employed in the treatment and rehabilitation of the person in recovery are included on this plan, and it thus takes on a key role in consolidating each team member's understanding of the purpose and importance of each modality and service. This is seen as crucial to maximally engaging the person in recovery in his or her rehabilitation and ensuring high fidelity implementation of the treatment plan. As the treatment plan is implemented, the focus of counseling turns to appraisal and evaluation of progress, with the ongoing objective of reinforcing the person's experience of success and self-efficacy. Counseling continues until the treatment plan goals have been met and recovery is well underway.

4.1.3   Social Skills Training

Correctly conducted social skills training is an effective method for teaching people how to function better in interpersonal situations

This modality is familiar to many mental health professionals, having been widely applied to a variety of recipient populations. There are highly developed and manualized versions designed specifically for people who live with schizophrenia and related conditions. Original research studies and a meta-analysis of 27 controlled trials (Benton & Schroeder, 1990) are consistent in showing that formal social skills training improves personal and social functioning, reduces hospital recidivism, and moderates symptoms in people who live with schizophrenia.

Social skills training of the type known to be effective for people who live with schizophrenia is an energetic, highly structured, highly interactive group modality. It involves almost continuous use of role playing exercises, with all group members serving as observers and assistants when not actually role-playing. It is necessary for the therapist to engage the people participating in training and facilitate their active participation throughout treatment. Unfortunately, "social skills groups" in mental health settings are often quite a bit less than this. The availability of therapist training materials and related resources make it possible for most mental health settings to be able to provide high quality services, but only if the training is actually done and high fidelity to training precepts is assured by quality assurance mechanisms. Research has demonstrated that, in the case of the UCLA Social and Independent Living Skills series (which includes social skills training, independent living skills interventions, and illness/wellness management), fidelity to the treatment manual is significantly related to patient outcomes (Wallace et al., 1992).

4.1.4   Problem Solving Skills Training

A widely used social skills training format, developed and disseminated by the UCLA Center for Research On Treatment and Rehabilitation of Psychosis, uses the familiar interpersonal problem-solving technique (D'Zurilla, 1986, 1988; D'Zurrila & Goldfried, 1971), a classic CBT approach. The approach uses a heuristic model of problem-solving. The model has five stages: detection and identification of the problem, generation of possible solution scenarios, selection of a solution, implementation of the solution, and evaluation of the results. People who participate in therapy learn this model, and then apply it to problems they have identified in their own lives. The cognitive and behavioral skills relevant to each stage are specifically rehearsed. It is generally accepted that cognitive behavioral problem solving is a key component of social skills training. Therefore, in addition to forming the content of separate problem-solving groups, problem solving activities, using the five steps outlined above, are incorporated into all of the UCLA skills training packages.

4.1.5   Independent Living Skills Training

People who live with schizophrenia and related disorders often lose or fail to develop skills associated with routine daily living, such as basic personal healthcare, grooming and hygiene, keeping a daily schedule, housekeeping, cooking, management of personal funds, and using public resources (transportation, libraries, etc). Acquisition of these skills contributes heavily to the ability to live safely and comfortably as members of the community. The table below lists the training packages currently available through the UCLA group, who have been the leaders in developing this type of intervention.

People who participate in independent living skills training receive classroom instruction and in vivo coaching to establish the knowledge base and performance ability necessary to use specific skills. Empirical verification of the effectiveness of independent living skill training, in terms of increases in the skills taught, is provided by separate controlled trials (e.g., Liberman et al., 1998; Michie, Lindsay, & Smith, 1998), but is more commonly incorporated in assessments of more comprehensive rehabilitation programs that include or emphasize living skill training (e.g., Burns & Santos, 1995; Wallace & Liberman, 1985).

The UCLA Social and Independent Living Skills modules are widely used in the U. S. and have been translated into fifteen languages. They form the backbone of many inpatient and outpatient rehabilitation programs. In addition to the UCLA modules, other skills training interventions using a similar format have been developed by other groups. These include a self-esteem module (Lecomte, et al., 1999) and a sleep module (Holmes, et al., 1995).

Table 6
Skills Training Groups in the UCLA Social and Independent Living Skills Program

Medication management
Symptom management
Basic conversation skills
Recreation for leisure
Friendship and intimacy
Community re-entry
Involving families in services for the seriously mentally ill
Workplace fundamentals
Grooming and hygiene

4.1.6   Supported Employment and Occupational Skills Training

Until recently, most people with schizophrenia who expressed an interest in working were placed in sheltered workshops or other settings where the jobs were reserved for people with a mental illness. This is known as the "train-place" model, because the idea was that vocational rehabilitation would eventually lead to placement in a real-world job. Times have changed, and efforts are now made to place people in real-world community job settings that match their interests, and to provide them with supports necessary to succeed. This practice, based on a "place-train" model, is known as supported employment. The rationale for supported employment includes several factors, such as: (1) a 10%–20% rate of competitive employment among people with serious mental illness (schizophrenia and and bipolar disorder), which speaks to the failure of traditional vocational programs to place people in real-world jobs; (2) most clients with serious mental illness want to work; (3) people with schizophrenia who return to work experience benefits in terms of symptom reduction and improved quality of life; and (4) several factors interfere with the ability to work, including cognitive impairment, psychotic symptoms, and negative symptoms. Supported employment emphasizes rapid job search and attainment by matching clients who want to work to jobs based on their interests and skills, rather than teaching them new skills to prepare for future jobs. These programs do not involve sheltered workshops and work enclaves, which typically pay below minimum wage and lack community integration (Mueser et al. 2004). Supported employment has demonstrated superiority to day treatment, group skills training, sheltered workshops, and psychosocial rehabilitation programs based on prevocational training, in terms of helping people get competitive paid employment (see Section 4.3, Efficacy, below).

There are several major differences between supported employment and traditional vocational rehabilitation. In supported employment, jobs are held by the client, not the program. Jobs can be held as long as the client can do the job. In addition, in supported employment, jobs are the responsibility of the client, not the mental health program, and jobs are rarely filled by another client after he or she leaves the job.

With supported employment, employment specialists serve on clients' treatment teams alongside other members of the team, including case managers and psychiatrists, in order to integrate vocational services with psychiatric treatment. Each employment specialist provides the full range of vocational services to each client, including engagement in services, identifying job interests and vocational assessment, job finding, and job support. Supported employment uses assertive outreach, based on the assertive community treatment (ACT) case management model, to deliver most vocational services in clients' natural settings in the community rather than at mental health or rehabilitation agencies (Mueser et al. 2004).

The Substance Abuse and Mental Health Services Administration (SAMHSA) has put forth six principles of supported employment. These are are as follows: (1) Eligibility for supported employment is based on consumer choice. No one is excluded who wants to participate. (2) Supported employment is integrated with treatment. Employment specialists coordinate plans with the treatment team: the case manager, therapist, psychiatrist, etc. (3) Competitive employment is the goal. The focus is community jobs anyone can apply for that pay at least minimum wage, including part-time and full-time jobs. (4) Job search starts soon after a consumer expresses interest in working. There are no requirements for completing extensive pre-employment assessment and training, or intermediate work experiences (like prevocational work units, transitional employment, or sheltered workshops). (5) Follow-along supports are continuous. Individualized supports to maintain employment continue as long as consumers want/need them. (6) Consumer preferences are important. Choices and decisions about work and support are individualized based on the person's preferences, strengths, and experiences.

In addition to supported employment, many people diagnosed with schizophrenia need help with general occupational skills, which are typically understood to be those that are important for *any* work-related activity, e.g., punctuality, proper workplace grooming, staying on task, following instructions, managing relationships with coworkers and supervisors. These should not be confused with vocational skills, which are more specific to particular kinds of work. Research generally supports the effectiveness of occupational skill training for increasing work-related performance (Durham, 1997; Wallace & Tauber, 2004) in people diagnosed with schizophrenia. A recently developed, manualized skills training package, the Workplace Fundamentals Module (Wallace, Tauber, & Wilde, 1999) can be used in a wide variety of settings to help improve basic occupational skills. In addition to general workplace skills, it is important to recognize that a variety of basic interpersonal skills are prerequisites to vocational functioning, and these are addressed by social, occupational, and independent living skills training.

SAMHSA has produced a package for public dissemination of supported employment practices. The package includes manuals and related materials for developing a supported employment program in conjunction with a comprehensive psychiatric rehabilitation service array. This represents a best practices exemplar for supported employment services.

4.1.7 Illness/Wellness Management Skill Training

Gaining the ability to manage one's own psychiatric illness is central to the rehabilitation and recovery perspective (Mueser, et al., 2002). In the rehabilitation literature, skill training in illness/wellness management has gradually differentiated itself from related social and living skills approaches, reflecting a growing recognition that specialized skills are needed to self-manage psychiatric disorders, comparable to skills needed to self-manage severe and persistent physical conditions such as diabetes. People learn about the episodic and persistent symptoms of their illness, the relationship between these symptoms and functional impairments, pharmacological and other techniques (e.g., relaxation and stress management) for controlling the symptoms, drug side effects, identification of "warning signs" of an impending relapse, and various other aspects of their disorder and its management. Behavioral skills indirectly relevant to disorder management are included, for example, the assertive skills necessary for dealing with the doctor and the doctor's receptionist in getting an appointment for a medication review.

Illness management is a critical part of psychiatric rehabilitation and recovery-oriented care

Illness/wellness management skill training materials have been packaged for testing and dissemination by several developer groups. A number of original studies and reviews confirm the effectiveness of skill training focused on illness/wellness management for improving adherence to treatment in people who live with severe mental illness (Conley & Kelly, 2001; Dolder, et al., 2003; Eckman et al., 1992; Heinssen, 2002; Ikebuchi & Anzai, 1995; Liberman, et al., 2002; Siddle & Kingdon, 2000; Velligan, et al., 2003; Young, et al., 1999; Zygmunt, Olfson, Boyer, & Mechanic, 2002). The SAMHSA (2004) has produced two packages for public dissemination that fall under this category, Illness Management and Recovery, and Medication Management Approaches in Psychiatry. Both packages include materials for all participants in the illness/wellness management process, including the person in recovery, medication prescriber, other service providers, family and friends. Together the two packages are exemplars of best practice in illness management skill training.

4.1.8 Peer Support

Peer support and self-help groups have been associated with the recovery movement throughout its recent history. One exemplar is Recovery Inc., for which there is some research evidence of benefit (Galanter, 1988). Another peer-based intervention involves the development of a Wellness Recovery Action Plan (WRAP) (Copeland, 1999). WRAP is a self-help life management system developed in 1997 by a group of people who had been working to recover from mental health difficulties and move forward with their lives. The goal of WRAP groups is for each participant to develop their own plan, or "toolbox," to maintain wellness. This includes daily maintenance activities that maintain wellness, recognition of personal triggers, early warning signs, signs that things have gotten worse when you can still do something about it, and a personal intensive crisis plan (including advance directives).

Some versions of assertive community treatment (e.g., Allness & Knoedler, 2003) include peer specialists. A controlled trial of a peer support and self-help group approach for people with severe affective disorders showed benefits in numerous domains of illness/wellness management and general well-being (Powell, et al., 2000). A partially controlled quasi-experimental trial found similar benefits by adding "peer specialists" to an intensive case management team (Felton, 1995). Although the data are promising, there is also evidence that the benefits of peer support and self-help approaches are heavily moderated by the "fit" between the person in recovery and the rest of the group (Luke, Roberts, & Rappaport, 1994). The outcome data do not yet meet the criteria for evidence-based practice, but research is ongoing and such data are expected to be forthcoming. In this sense, peer support and self-help approaches are "promising practices."

It is important to note that peer support and self-help reflect more than a specific approach to illness/wellness management. In the rehabilitation and re-covery perspective, peer involvement, social support, and nonprofessional help are important in most, if not all services and domains. As models for peer in-volvement continue to evolve, they may fit under a number of evidence-based practice rubrics in addition to illness/wellness management.

4.1.9 Family Consultation, Education, and Therapy

A broad spectrum of family processes and therapies have long been of interest in schizophrenia research. In the 1950s, many believed that families, and parents in particular, played a causal role in the etiology of the disorder. This view was never empirically supported and today is largely discredited. Nevertheless, fam-ily members often experience guilt and/or distress in this regard. Clinicians should always be vigilant for this possibility and intervene with corrective in-formation when indicated.

In a number of controlled outcome trials, family services that include psy-choeducation, reduction of expressed emotion via teaching of communication skills, behavioral management, and social support have been found to reduce relapse and recidivism rates (reviewed by Pilling, Bebbington, Kuipers, & Garety, 2002; Lam, 1991). These approaches can also benefit the family as a whole by reducing disruption of activities, physical and mental health prob-lems, and subjective burden (Falloon & Pederson, 1985). A variant of this approach to family services uses multifamily psychoeducational groups to build supportive social networks (McFarlane, Lukens, Link, Dushay, et al., 1995). In controlled comparative studies the multifamily format has been superior to a single-family format in reducing relapse (McFarlane, Link, Dushay, Marchal, et al., 1995). The SAMHSA (2004) has produced a package for public dissemination that falls under this category, Family Psychoeduca-tion. The package provides materials for general family education and sup-port programs.

Controlled trials of briefer family education and support modalities, ranging from one to eight sessions, have been found to increase family members' sense of support from the treatment team, increase their knowledge about schizophre-nia and its treatment and rehabilitation, improve their coping, reduce distress and self-blame, and increase satisfaction with services (Abramowitz & Coursey, 1989; Posner, Wilson, Kral, Lander, et al. 1992). However, the briefer modali-ties have not been shown to reduce relapse or hospital recidivism, in contrast to family-based treatments of longer duration.

4.1.10 Contingency Management

Contingency management is a genre of techniques that evolved from learning and social learning theories in the 1960s. They are especially important in psychiatric inpatient settings (see Corrigan & Liberman, 1994). As community-based programs for people with schizophrenia have proliferated, relevance of contingency management to such programs has generalized. Nevertheless, contingency management is one of the most underutilized technologies in adult mental health services. Implementation is complicated by the need for administrative mechanisms to review and approve individual treatment plans, because of the potentially restrictive nature of the approach and the fact that it is often used to address problems with people who are involuntary patients.

The earliest applications of contingency management for schizophrenia, in the form of token economies in psychiatric hospitals, provided strong empirical evidence of effectiveness in promoting adaptive behavior (Ayllon & Azrin, 1968, Paul & Lentz, 1977). In addition to general effects on maladaptive and adaptive behavior, when combined with other social-learning modalities, contingency management has been shown to be effective with two of the most troublesome and drug-resistant problems encountered in inpatient settings, aggression (Beck, et al., 1991) and polydipsia (Baldwin, et al., 1992). As psychiatric rehabilitation has evolved, the role of contingency management in enhancing engagement in rehabilitation activities has become increasingly important (Heinssen, 2002).

4.1.11 Individual Psychotherapy

Cognitive Behavior Therapy (CBT)

CBT is a type of psychotherapy, based on principles of conditioning, learning, and cognition. As applied to schizophrenia, CBT engages patients in collaboratively challenging their interpretations of events or experiences. It is thus often used to assist patients in developing more realistic alternatives to delusional and paranoid thinking. It can also be used to help patients develop less stressful attributions for hallucinations. In the case of negative symptoms, CBT is often used to challenge anhedonic beliefs, to schedule activities, and to administer self-rewards for increasingly engaging in pleasurable activities. CBT works best with patients who are willing to actively participate in the treatment, often as the result of distress from symptoms and/or at least minimal insight into the abnormal nature of their experiences.

> CBT adapted for psychotic patients can help reduce delusional thinking, paranoia, distress from hallucinations, and negative symptoms

A meta-analysis of CBT for schizophrenia, including 7 randomized controlled trials (Rector & Beck, 2001), showed that CBT produced large clinical effects on both positive and negative symptoms. CBT as an adjunct to routine clinical care also resulted in significant additional benefits compared with routine clinical care plus supportive therapy. An updated review of 17 clinical trials testing effectiveness of CBT for schizophrenia (Dickerson, 2004) showed that CBT results in better outcomes on specific measures compared with routine care or supportive therapies in a variety of settings (e.g., day-treatment programs, long-stay inpatient programs) and across some special patient populations (e.g., relapse-vulnerable patients, older adults with schizophrenia, individuals with comorbid substance abuse or anxiety disorders). There is also preliminary evidence that these improvements translate into improved social functioning (Temple & Ho, 2005). The specific symptoms shown to be alleviated with adjunctive CBT include delusions, distress or delusions related to auditory hallucinations (AH), paranoia and negative symptoms (Beck & Rector, 2005; Rector & Beck, 2001). Improvements in distress related to AH and delusions are maintained at follow-up.

In addition to problems uniquely associated with psychotic disorders, various forms of CBT are effective for addressing generalized anxiety, panic, social anxiety, depression, obsessive-compulsive symptoms, and substance abuse. These problems often co-occur with chronic psychotic disorders, and there is no reason to believe that CBT interventions are any less effective in treating them in people with schizophrenia than in the general population.

CBT for psychosis grew out of earlier work on CBT for other disorders and followed a strict cognitive model. It is increasingly recognized, however, that CBT for psychosis is evolving. For example, Chadwick et al. (1996) described how symptom expression often occurs during periods of anxiety, in situations where there is a threat to the self. They recommend that incorporating this insight into intervention refinement be undertaken. Dreams are also increasingly being used in CBT in general, and can be viewed as expressing important statements about cognitive and affective schemata (Beck, 1971; Rosner et al., 2004). The use of dreams in a constructivist sense as metaphors for exploring patients' sensory, emotional, and cognitive experiences has not yet been systematically used in CBT for psychosis. However, use of hallucinations as metaphorical experiences (Silverstein, in press) suggests that this may be a fruitful technique for patients who are able to engage in it.

Psychoanalysis and Psychoanalytic Therapies

Psychodynamic therapies for schizophrenia vary somewhat in their goals and technique, but, as discussed by Bachmann et al. (2003), agree on the following principles:

1. Psychotherapy with schizophrenia patients is possible;
2. The classic psychoanalytic approach (including free association and having the patient lying prone on a couch with the therapist out of sight) is contraindicated;
3. The present should be emphasized over the past;
4. Interpretations should only be used with caution;
5. Goals are (a) experience of the self and the therapist as two separate people that share a relationship, (b) stabilization of ego-boundaries and identity, and (c) integration of the psychotic experience;
6. The frequency of sessions should range from 1–3 sessions per week, and be conducted for a minimum of two years; and
7. Therapists who work with schizophrenia patients need to have a high level of frustration tolerance and not have a need to derive narcissistic gratification from the patient's efforts or progress.

With the advent of the biological revolution in psychiatry, and given the negative findings of influential studies of psychoanalytic therapy outcome in schizophrenia (e.g., Gunderson et al., 1984), psychodynamic therapies for schizophrenia came under attack as being not helpful, and possibly harmful (Drake & Sederer, 1986). In 1998, a major paper on treatment recommendations by the

Psychodynamic therapy should only be attempted with stable patients and by experienced therapists

Schizophrenia Patient Outcome Research Team (PORT), stated that "psychotherapies adhering to a psychodynamic model . . . should not be used" ((Lehman et al., 1998, p. 7). Meta-analyses of psychotherapy in schizophrenia, however, indicate that this negative conclusion may be premature. For example, Mojtabai et al. (1998) reported that psychodynamic therapies did not produce poorer outcomes than other forms of individual therapy for schizophrenia. Karon and VandenBos (1981) found that while overall, psychodynamic psychotherapy added little to treatment with medication, patients of experienced therapists improved significantly more than patients of less experienced therapists, or those on medication alone. Similar findings were reported from a reanalysis of the Boston Psychotherapy Study (Gunderson et al., 1984; Glass et al., 1989), at least in terms of improvement in negative symptoms. An important factor in determining patient suitability for psychodynamic psychotherapy, however, may be the stability of the patient. A recent study (Hauff et al. 2002) indicated that while inpatients with schizophrenia who were more stable at the initiation of treatment improved over time, those who were functioning more poorly at the beginning of treatment deteriorated after the onset of therapy. In summary, there is research indicating that psychodynamic psychotherapies can be beneficial for patients with schizophrenia, but mainly for more stable patients, and when delivered by therapists experienced with these approaches. Much more research on the effectiveness of these therapies is needed, however, because many past studies were methodologically flawed, including using outcomes that had questionable relevance to the goals of the treatment (Diamond et al., 1997).

Personal Therapy

Personal therapy (Hogarty, 2003; Hogarty, et al., 1997) is another form of individual psychotherapy for chronic psychotic disorders. Its focus on cognition is similar to CBT, but its overall emphasis is more on personal and social functioning rather than specific symptoms and behaviors. Although the Hogarty group has produced compelling evidence for effectiveness, controlled trials have not been replicated by other research groups. In that sense, personal therapy is therefore best described as a "promising" practice. However, personal therapy is very similar to CBT for persons diagnosed with schizophrenia, and in this sense it can be considered a variant of an evidence-based practice.

Acute Treatment, Crisis Intervention, and Related Services

There is general agreement that the availability of acute inpatient and/or crisis/respite services is a necessary component of a mental health service system for people with schizophrenia. However, there is some room for debate about the precise nature of crisis intervention services.

One view that has been dominant since the 1960s is that crises in schizophrenia are predominantly the result of psychotic relapse, and the best setting in which to evaluate and treat psychotic relapse is in an inpatient psychiatric unit. Psychiatric inpatient units do provide necessary safety and medical care, but they are not necessarily the most cost-effective alternative. Crises in schizophrenia may be driven by a host of factors other than psychotic relapse, and in such cases addressing those factors in a timely way may be more important than removing the person to a protected environment and administering drugs. As a result, alternative crisis services and 24-hour respite facilities are increasingly included in mental health systems (Brook, 1973; Campos & Gieser, 1985). Often, these are incorporated in a comprehensive case management system. Recent research on a crisis hostel program that includes peer involvement and psychosocial approaches provides evidence for subjective and economic benefits (Dumont and Jones, 2001). Controlled research on crisis hostels has not reached the level of evidence-based practice, but the existing research and the social value of consumer involvement identify crisis hostels and related alternatives to acute inpatient hospitalization as promising practices.

Another predominant view has been that however useful psychosocial treatment may be in the residual phase, pharmacotherapy is the sole treatment of choice for acute psychosis. This presumption is challenged by a twelve year study of drug-free treatment, the Soteria Project (reviewed by Mosher, 1999). In a series of controlled studies, the drug-free condition proved comparable to conventional hospital-and-medication treatment for a large majority of recipients. The drug-free treatment was also considerably less expensive. Strauss and Carpenter (Strauss & Carpenter, 1977) also reported successful treatment of acute schizophrenia without drugs.

The Soteria project successfully treated young people with schizophrenia without medication, in a specialized residential setting

Despite these findings, drug-free treatment of schizophrenia, especially in the acute phase, remains outside generally accepted standards of practice. While caution about drug-free treatment is clearly indicated, the available data exacerbate suspicions that treatment of people who are diagnosed with schizophrenia has become overly dependent on psychopharmacology, even in the acute phase.

Specialized Integrated Treatment for Co-occurring Substance Abuse

Co-occurring substance abuse is a widely recognized problem in schizophrenia, and is a cause of relapse and a barrier to rehabilitation and recovery. Conventional substance abuse approaches, such as 12-step programs, are effective for some people, and should be included in a service array. In addition, many people who live with SMI benefit from specialized programs specifically designed to address substance abuse within the context of psychiatric rehabilitation programming (Drake, et al., 1998; Drake & Mueser, 2000, 2001; Kavanagh, et al., 2002).

Standard current practice for schizophrenia patients with substance abuse disorders is to have both problems treated at the same time by the same treatment team

The Substance Abuse and Mental Health Services Administration (SAMHSA, 2004) has produced a package for public dissemination that falls under this category, co-occurring disorders: Integrated Dual Disorders Treatment. The package includes manuals and related materials for developing integrated substance abuse treatment in conjunction with a comprehensive psychiatric rehabilitation service array. The package represents a best practices exemplar for dual disorder services. As noted above, the UCLA group has also developed an effective form of integrated dual disorder treatment, the Substance Abuse Management Module (Shaner et al., 2003).

Cognitive Rehabilitation

Because traditional antipsychotic medications have had minimal or sometimes deleterious effects on cognition after the acute phase (Corrigan & Penn, 1995), these cannot be considered adequate methods to improve cognitive functioning. For the most part, even atypical antipsychotic medications have not demonstrated significant effects on cognition, with positive findings being generally associated with small effect sizes, and offset by an almost equal number of published negative findings (Carpenter & Gold, 2002; Harvey & Keefe, 2001; Meltzer & McGurk, 1999). Moreover, neither first- nor second-generation medications improve social and role functioning in schizophrenia, even when demonstrating significant improvement in symptomatology and cognition (Bellack et al., 2004; Harvey et al. 2003b; Rifkin et al., 1979). All of these data suggest that additional interventions are needed to enhance cognitive functioning.

One approach to treating neurocognitive deficits involves the adaptation of methods from experimental and clinical psychology. For example, while dichotic listening procedures have been used to demonstrate auditory selective attention deficits in schizophrenia, they have also been adapted to enable patients to practice attending to relevant stimuli and ignoring irrelevant stimuli (e.g., Spaulding et al., 1986; Hatashita-Wong & Silverstein, 2003). This technique helps patients cope with the distracting effects of auditory hallucinations.

Another recent approach utilizes computers to administer tasks based on neuropsychological tests or exercises developed for remediation of cognitive deficits in learning disabilities (Brieff, 1994). Studies using a neuropsychological educational approach to rehabilitation (NEAR) (e.g., Medalia, et al., 1998; 2001; Medalia, Dorn, & Watras-Gans, 2000; Medalia & Revheim, 1998; Medalia, Revheim, & Casey, 2000) rely heavily on computer-assisted training. A core aspect of the NEAR model is the use of educational techniques designed to facilitate learning by increasing intrinsic motivation and task engagement. Examples of techniques used to accomplish these goals are contextualization of the learning activity in real-world situations, multisensory stimulation, personalization of and control over the learning activity, and the use of opportunities to use information actively (Medalia & Revheim, 1998). Data indicate that use of the NEAR model in outpatient and chronic inpatient settings was associated with enjoyment of the training, cognitive improvement, and gains on independent measures of problem solving (Medalia, Revheim, & Casey, 2000). Another study demonstrated improved problem-solving in acute schizophrenia patients, as well as improvements in the ability to cope with symptoms and to modify the impression made on others (Medalia, Dorn, & Watras-Gans, 2000).

A group-based approach to cognitive rehabilitation is integrated psychological therapy (IPT) (Brenner, Hodel, Roder, & Corrigan, 1992; Brenner, et al., 1994). This intervention targets skills in a hierarchical fashion, beginning with conceptual differentiation (executive functioning), and moving through social perception, verbal communication, basic social skills, and interpersonal problem solving segments. Skills are targeted through group practice and problem solving using a series of exercises that increase in complexity over time. Results from studies of IPT have been mixed (Brenner, et al., 1992, 1994; Spaulding, et al., 1999a, 1999b). In Brenner's studies, some cognitive effects were found, along with little evidence of generalizability of the effects to real-world behavior. Spaulding et al. (1999a, 1999b) reported an additive effect of cognitive rehabilitation above social-learning based milieu treatment on cognitive functioning, and improvement on a measure of social cognition, suggesting that changes in social functioning may result from IPT. Approaches similar to IPT have been developed for use in individual treatment sessions (e.g., van der Gaag, 1992, Wykes, Reeder, Corner, Williams, & Everitt, 1999).

Hogarty and Flesher (1999a, 1999b) developed a treatment called cognitive enhancement therapy (CET). This approach was developed for use with outpatient populations. It is theoretically tied to developmental models of schizophrenia, and therefore conceptualizes many of the deficits patients have in terms of their failures to develop age appropriate cognitive and social cognitive skills. A recent controlled study of CET with a large sample of patients demonstrated effectiveness and maintenance of gains over a one year period (Hogarty et al., 2004).

Some researchers have suggested utilizing approaches that focus on helping patients manage cognitively demanding tasks in the real world (Flesher, 1990; Hogarty & Flesher, 1999a, b; Velligan & Bow-Thomas, 2000). One such approach is Cognitive Adaptation Training (CAT) which involves the use of cues and compensating features in the patient's environment (Velligan & Bow-Thomas, 2000). As the authors note, CAT has more in common with case management than with traditional cognitive rehabilitation, in that it involves home visits and in-vivo supports, and it not viewed as a method for strengthening/restoring cognitive functions or their neural correlates. Preliminary data on this approach are encouraging.

Cognitive rehabilitation can help to restore functioning and to help patients compensate for their deficits

An ongoing problem in the field of cognitive rehabilitation is that many interventions are not appropriate for the patients with most severe attentional impairment. This is because these patients (who often have attention spans of under five minutes) can not attend to the material presented to them for any significant length of time, and exercises targeting higher level cognitive skills such as executive functioning may lead to clinical deterioration in patients with impairments in more basic functions such as sustained attention (see Silverstein, Menditto, & Stuve, 1999, 2001). For this group, improvements have been reported using the behavioral technique of shaping. Shaping is a method to achieve operant conditioning, and (duration of) attentive behavior frequently is a specifically targeted response. The primary technique involved is differential reinforcement of successive approximations to the final target behavior. For example, rather than waiting for the complete behavior (e.g., a 30-minute attention span) to occur before offering reinforcement, reinforcement is provided for successive approximations or small steps toward the final behavior. When the initial step toward a behavior (e.g., three minutes of continuous attention) has been reinforced and occurs fairly regularly, the criterion for reinforcement is raised to a more challenging level (e.g., four minutes of continuous attention), and so on.

A number of published reports have demonstrated the effectiveness of shaping techniques for improving duration of on-task behavior in inpatients with chronic schizophrenia that had been considered treatment refractory (Bellus et al., 1999; Menditto et al., 1991; Silverstein et al., 1998b, 1999; Spaulding et al., 1986). In a recent study, Silverstein et al. (2005a) demonstrated that whereas a form of attention training developed for brain injured patients had little effect on actual attentiveness in skills training groups, a manualized attention shaping procedure wherein patient goals for attentiveness during skills training groups were individualized led to dramatic improvements compared to a control group.

Attention shaping approaches have dramatically increased attentiveness in rehabilitation interventions among the most severely ill patients

A technique similar to shaping is known as errorless learning (O'Carroll, et al., 1999). Errorless learning involves beginning training on tasks where there is a high expectation of success and proceeding through a graded series of tasks that become increasingly more complex. The goal of this procedure is to minimize the commission of errors while at the same time achieving performance mastery. Once a given level of performance is achieved, tasks at the next level of complexity are introduced. Errorless learning has demonstrated effectiveness in the treatment of developmentally disabled and neurologically impaired individuals (Baddeley, 1992; Kern, 1996). Moreover, it has been used as a technique to improve the performance of people with schizophrenia on neuropsychological tests of attention, memory (Bellack, et al., 1996; Benedict, et al., 1994; O'Carroll et al., 1999; Stratta, et al., 1994; Summerfelt, et al., 1991a, 1999b; Vollema, Guertsen, & Van Voorst, 1995; Wexler, et al., 1997) and executive functioning (Kern et al., 1996), to treat executive functioning impairments within the context of a larger neurocognitive rehabilitation program (Wykes, et al., 1999), and to improve vocational functioning (Kern et al., 2002, 2003) and problem solving abilities (Kern et al., 2005).

Supported cognition integrates neuropsychological and behavioral approaches to improve performance in real-world settings

Evidence from the fields of behavioral treatment, social skills training, academic intervention, and cognitive rehabilitation of TBI patients, on training and transfer of behavioral and cognitive skills suggests that interventions are effective to the extent that they are embedded within activities and settings that are meaningful to the person receiving them (reviewed in Ylvisaker et al. 2003). This has led to an increased emphasis on "supported cognition" interventions that integrate neuropsychological and behavioral approaches (Cicerone et al. 2000; Feeney & Ylvisaker, 2003). Attention shaping is consistent with this approach. That delivery of a cognitive intervention concurrently with a skills-based intervention can be effective in schizophrenia is supported by recent findings that combining cognitive remediation with vocational rehabilitation leads to greater improvements in neuropsychological test performance (Bell, Bryson, & Wexler, 2003), and improved work attendance and performance (Fiszdon & Bell, 2004) compared to vocational rehabilitation alone. Support for an integrated approach also comes from studies of errorless learning in schizophrenia. It should be noted that this approach is also consistent with the general trend in schizophrenia treatment toward "place-train" interventions, and these have been found to produce improved outcomes in the domains of vocational (Mueser et al. 2004) and social (Davidson et al. 2004) functioning.

Finally, with the increased focus recently on social cognition as an important treatment target in schizophrenia (Green et al., 2005), rehabilitation efforts are being developed for social cognitive functions. This work is in its infancy, but early efforts are demonstrating promise. For example, Wolwer et al. (2005) demonstrated that while traditional cognitive rehabilitation did not improve facial affect processing in schizophrenia, a new program called Tackling Affect Recognition (TAR) improved performance to that of normal controls in past studies.

4.1.12 Supported Housing

Recent years have seen an increased availability of supported housing. One element of the supported housing movement is a change from reliance on a faculty-based residential treatment setting or a series of such specialized settings as the focus for treatment and rehabilitation to the need for a safe, secure home of one's own as a basis for a stable life in the community. In this new paradigm, professionals no longer select the setting or determine what type of placement is best for the patient, nor do they place a person on the basis of open beds or slots in the residential service system. Rather, consistent with a recovery-oriented philosophy, the person is helped to choose an appropriate living situation on the basis of personal criteria, preferences, resources, and needs. As such, the patient assumes the role of tenant, householder, neighbor, and mainstream community member, working together with staff on mutually agreed on goals and tasks geared toward the individual's success and stability in the home chosen. Additionally, social support, case management, crisis intervention, in-home skills training, and accessible psychiatric consultation, are flexibly wrapped around the changing needs of the patient. Financial assistance is available through subsidized rental vouchers (Section 8 grants) provided by the U. S. Department of Housing and Urban Development.

Three large research efforts have provided information on the value of the supported housing approach (Lipton et al., 2000). These demonstration projects indicate that innovative, supportive housing programs do seem to allow many persons with long-term psychiatric disorders to develop a stable home in the community. Supported housing can, therefore, be considered an evidence based practice. On the other hand, the data indicate that an ambitious policy of independent housing, without consideration of such factors as substance abuse, an individual's social network, poverty, quality of housing, criminal activity in the neighborhood, and the amount and quality of ongoing, personalized support and assistance from community-based mental health teams, is not likely to maintain long-term residential stability.

Supported housing is an effective intervention, if embedded within comprehensive rehabilitation services

4.1.13 Specialized Models for Service Integration and Provision

Specialized models for integrated provision of psychiatric treatment and rehabilitation have evolved in response to the needs of people with especially severe disabilities associated with schizophrenia. Three models supported by outcome data are the psychosocial clubhouse model, assertive community treatment, and residential social learning programs.

Psychosocial Clubhouse Model
Psychosocial Clubhouse models include a number of specific approaches. The key common element is a social club-like administrative organization, emphasis on peer support, an organized community of participants, a physical residential or occupational setting or both. Evidence-based exemplars include Fairweather Lodge (Fairweather, Sanders, Maynard & Cressler, 1969) and Thresholds (Bond, Dincin, Setze & Witheridge, 1984). Today, specific treatment and rehabilitation services are often provided through some form of clubhouse model, including social, living and occupational skill training, in residential settings (e.g., group homes) and day rehabilitation programs. Both residential and day rehabilitation clubhouse programs provide important sites for skill training, therapy, rehabilitation counseling, peer support groups and other rehabilitation/recovery services. The service array may or may not be comprehensive, and may or may not include treatment planning and case management. If not comprehensive, specific services are coordinated with other providers. Clubhouse models generally emphasize consumer involvement and peer support, and are in that sense especially consistent with the social values associated with rehabilitation and recovery.

Assertive Community Treatment
Assertive community treatment (ACT, also known as Programs of ACT, PACT) is a comprehensive approach to services for people who live with severe and

Assertive community treatment is superior to case management in many respects, but is much less available

disabling psychiatric disorders (Test & Stein, 1976). In addition to case management, ACT programs include conventional psychiatric services and varying amounts of rehabilitative services, delivered in an outreach mode that takes the services to the person. Compared to case management (CM) and intensive case management (ICM) services, ACT teams deliver services while CM and ICM workers link patients to other service providers; ACT teams share caseloads, whereas traditional case managers usually have caseloads greater than 30 (although less with ICM); ACT involves daily team meetings; and ACT has established guidelines, promoting fidelity across sites.

At least one version of ACT has been commercially packaged as a proprietary product (Allness & Knoedler, 2003) and a second has been produced for public dissemination by the SAMHSA (2004). By following the manual and using the materials, which include quality assurance and program evaluation tools, treatment teams can credibly provide services according to a standard model (fidelity to the model is a key issue in research and implementation, as versions of ACT can be quite different).

There has been much research on the efficacy and cost-effectiveness of ACT programs, but the results are complex (reviewed by Mueser, et al. 1998; Burns & Santos, 1995; Burns, Creed, Fahy, Thompson, Tyrer & Whie, 1999; Monroe-DeVita and Mohatt, 1999; Byford et al., 2000; Burns, Fioritti, Holloway, Malm & Rossler, 2001). Approximately 5%–20% of patients with serious mental illness (at least half of whom are diagnosed with schizophrenia) do not function well in ACT, but the reasons for this are unclear. Although the effects of ACT on rehospitalization are relatively robust, it is unclear whether there is a reliable improvement in people's social and personal functioning. Effectiveness appears to be influenced by moderating factors such as the amount of skill training included, various consumer characteristics and the treatment team's control over hospitalization. The transition from institution to community is enhanced by inclusion of focused skill training with case management (MacKain, Smith, Wallace, & Kopelowicz, 1998).

Social Learning Program

Many treatment elements can be easily integrated within the original SLP framework

The Social Learning Program (SLP) is a comprehensive, integrated network of learning-based techniques and skills-training technologies delivered by all staff within the context of a supportive, rehabilitation-oriented inpatient program. As noted elsewhere in this book, research indicates that SLP is the most effective form of inpatient treatment for people with schizophrenia, including so-called "treatment-refractory" patients. The SLP has demonstrated effectiveness with a wide range of disabled people in a variety of settings (e.g., state and private hospitals, maximum-security forensic hospitals). The components of the SLP form an extremely positive teaching environment that assists clients in developing adaptive behaviors and skills relevant to successful return to the community. Contemporary versions of this approach incorporate skills training technologies, psychiatric rehabilitation techniques for engaging clients, cognitive-behavior therapy, vocational rehabilitation, cognitive rehabilitation, and substance abuse treatment (Menditto, 2002; Paul & Menditto, 1992; Paul, Stuve, & Menditto, 1997).

Comprehensive SLP's include a number of key factors critical to their success, including:

(a) Rehabilitation Philosophy and Values. A fundamental assumption of this approach is that all persons with severe mental disorders, no matter how severely impaired, can learn new behaviors and skills. Moreover, by acquiring the relevant skills and developing adequate environmental supports, individuals with severe mental disorders can return to communities of their choice where they can live successful and satisfying lives.

(b) Learning-Based Techniques. The SLP incorporates a wide variety of techniques based on fundamental learning principles. Differential reinforcement forms the basis of many of the procedures of the SLP. Staff of all levels and disciplines are highly trained and carefully supervised in the timely and consistent delivery of verbal praise, positive social attention, and material reinforcement to adaptive behaviors while applying extinction or response-cost techniques to bizarre, aggressive, or rule-violating behaviors. The result is a highly reinforcing, positive, and supportive environment.

(c) Direct Skills Training. The SLP incorporates a diverse array of skills training, cognitive remediation, vocational training and psychoeducational components within a highly structured schedule. Groups and classes include training in skills directly relevant to community living such as: social skills, problem solving, anger management, functional living skills, academic needs, relapse prevention, leisure skills, and self management. Individuals who have such severe cognitive impairments as to make it difficult for them to participate in regular classes and groups are enrolled in special shaping classes two or three times a day, five days a week, as described above.

(d) Token Economy. While most comprehensive SLP's include some sort of token economy or point system to reinforce clients for working on skill development, attending and participating in classes and groups, accomplishing specific behavioral targets, etc., some do not, relying instead exclusively on individual behavioral contracts, contingency management plans, or social reinforcement. In all well designed SLP's, specific objectives and goals of clients are individualized as are the specific interventions for assisting them with acquiring the skills necessary to accomplish these goals/objectives. SLP's should not rely on contrived reinforcers (e.g., tokens) unnecessarily, nor apply reinforcement systems in simplistic, "one-size fits all" manner. Furthermore, programs that do include such systems of reinforcement should incorporate the systematic withdrawal of tokens or points with an emphasis on generalization training so that clients will be able to apply acquired skills and knowledge successfully in "real life" community settings under more natural reinforcement conditions.

(e) Assessment Systems. Three direct observational assessment systems, the TSBC, CFRS, and SRIC support the operations of the SLP, providing most of the information necessary to make clinical decisions about individual clients as well as to evaluate the integrity and effectiveness of the program. These instruments are discussed above in the section on assessment.

(f) Staff Training and Supervision. Given the complexity, specificity, and range of procedures involved in the SLP, staff training is of paramount importance. All staff are involved in extensive initial and ongoing training, employing an integrated-technical approach that includes didactic instruction with in vivo practice (Jones,

Menditto, Geeson, Larson, & Sadewhite, 2001). Competency-based supervision is provided through regular performance feedback using data from the SRIC as well as structured supervisory observations (Stuve & Menditto, 1999).

(g) Continuum of Care. As individuals acquire skills and develop goals for community living, it is critical that they be afforded opportunities to apply these skills and pursue their goals in community settings with ongoing declining contact after-care. Clients may require various levels of support from structured residential services to supported employment to practicing skills in community settings. To the extent that staff providing this support are familiar with social learning principles and procedures or at least receive consultation in such, the transitions for clients are smoother and more effective. Thus, SLP's arrange for such services through the operation of community based services and the provision of consultation and training to other community providers (Menditto, 2002).

Clubhouse models, ACT and residential social learning programs are evidence-based practices for cost-effective service provision, for overlapping ranges of individuals within the population of concern. Generally, clubhouse models are most cost-effective for people who have realized a substantial degree of stability, and are motivated for and invested in recovery. People whose disorder is less stable, have a higher level of disability and/or who are less able to sustain their engagement in rehabilitation and recovery, are expected to benefit more from ACT. There is a range of persons who, in the later stages of the process of recovery, require less service integration and support than clubhouse programs provide, and for them conventional case management is sufficient to coordinate needed services. At the other end of the continuum, a small but significant proportion of the population of concern, at an earlier stage of recovery, does not do well in clubhouse programs or ACT. Also, for legal and public safety reasons, some people cannot access clubhouse programs or ACT until later stages of recovery. For these people, the organizational model of residential social learning-based rehabilitation provides the best alternative. It is important to note, in this regard, that social learning programs' key outcome is their effectiveness at helping people move to less intensive/restrictive settings, including clubhouse and ACT programs and conventional case management.

Clubhouse, ACT and social learning programs are *organizational* models in which specific integrated treatment and rehabilitation is provided. All available outcome data indicate that the *content* of the services is as important as the organizational model. Use of any of the organizational models requires high-fidelity treatment planning and progress evaluation, and the full panoply of specific evidence-based practices. No organizational model is effective if there are insufficient services to organize.

4.2   Mechanisms of Action

Schizophrenia is a complex disorder and its comprehensive treatment requires intervention at multiple levels, typically including neurophysiological, cognitive, behavioral, environmental, family systems, and societal factors (e.g., efforts at stigma reduction, community provision of adequate medical and dental care and access to entitlements, appropriate housing, etc.) (Liberman, Kopelowicz, & Silverstein, 2005). Therefore, identifying mechanisms of change is likely to be equally daunting, although critical to designing improved services. Below, we discuss several factors that are likely to be involved in the normalization of functioning in people with schizophrenia.

First and foremost, it is important to recognize that variables that have been shown to be important for treatment outcome with psychiatric patients in general are also important to people with schizophrenia. These include the quality of the therapeutic alliance with caregivers (Saunders & Lueger, 2005), and the degree to which patients feel positively toward their treatment providers (Hall et al., 2002).

Recent work in the area of psychiatric rehabilitation has focused on specifying mechanisms involved in benefit from treatment. Several possible mechanisms of neurocognitive change in rehabilitation have been identified. One involves learning of new "compensatory metaskills," or ways to consciously think about how to think about situations. Symbol-coded procedural scripts enhance directed attention, collection of social information, recognition of situations, and problem-solving. These ideas form the core of Meichenbaum's (1969; Meichenbaum & Cameron, 1973) self-instructional training, which has demonstrated preliminary success in the treatment of schizophrenia. A second mechanism is extinction of self-protective cognitive avoidance responses. Avoidance is a preferred coping strategy among people with episodic psychosis, but they become less avoidant with rehabilitation (Böker & Brenner, 1983). A third mechanism involves normalization of neuroendocrine regulation of brain function. It is well known that consistent, diurnal environmental demand ("stress") reregulates HPA functioning, and that this has detrimental effects on cognition. However, skill training in self-regulation, and stress and illness management reduces stress, and improves general coping ability. This shifts HPA response from "stress" to "activation," and cognitive responsiveness improves. Fourth, positive treatment response may involve a reorganization of the cognitive and behavioral repertoire in response to environmental demand. Schizophrenia has been characterized by a "response-hierarchy collapse" (Broen, 1968; Broen & Storms. 1966) in that excess neurophysiological activation both increases the likelihood that normally nondominant response tendencies will be expressed, and that normally dominant responses will not be expressed. However, reestablishment of adaptive response hierarchies and patient accessibility to task-relevant skills can be enhanced by high redundancy, consistency, and a focus on basic adaptive functioning. All of these are characteristic of psychiatric rehabilitation programs and social learning programs, as discussed above.

Development of metacognitive skills, extinction of cognitive avoidance responses, and HPA axis regulation may underlie psychiatric rehabilitation

Mechanisms of change in CBT and other psychotherapies for schizophrenia are likely to involve the factors noted above. Interestingly, while models for cognitive therapy for psychosis originally focused on purely cognitive factors as mechanisms of change, these models are now becoming more sophisticated and are including concepts such as the self, and coordination of cognitive activity. For example, rather than focusing solely on factors such as changing inappropriate attributions, cognitive therapy for schizophrenia increasingly recognizes that stress and symptom expression are more likely to occur in situations where there is a threat to the self-system (Chadwick et al., 1996). Abnormalities in the experience of the self are prominent features of schizophrenia

(Danion et al., 1999; Lysaker & Lysaker, 2002, 2004; Sass, 1992; Sass & Parnas, 2003), and it is likely that future therapy development efforts will focus on techniques to improve self-integration.

Attention shaping approaches may exert their effects, not only through bottom-up improvements in attention and skill acquisition, but also through top-down effects resulting from improved performance, such as increases in self-efficacy, working alliance, treatment satisfaction, and intrinsic motivation (Silverstein & Wilkniss, 2004; Wilson, 1997; Ylvisaker et al. 2003). For example, recent work in the cognitive rehabilitation of TBI patients has increasingly recognized the need to move beyond an approach based solely in cognitive theory, and to address variables such as motivation and the therapist-client relationship (Wilson, 1997). In addition, "positive behavioral momentum" (Mace et al. 1997), which results from the experience of success in tasks following a gradient from easier to more difficult, is now considered a key factor in successful rehabilitation of TBI patients, and is a core feature of attention shaping. Also, evidence from nonclinical populations indicates that self-efficacy beliefs play a mediating role between task resources and task engagement: engagement increases efficacy beliefs, and this then increases resources devoted to the task (Llorents et al., in press). We hypothesize that this "positive gain spiral" (Llorents et al., in press) mechanism is operative in shaping. Further evidence on the effects of positive attitudes toward tasks comes from a recent study by Beas and Salanova (in press), who demonstrated that as task-related attitudes become more positive, perceived self-efficacy to perform the task increases. This is relevant to attention shaping because the social and material reinforcers associated with successful performance are hypothesized to enhance both positive feelings toward the treatment group and self-efficacy, which can lead to increased task resources, further success, further improvements in self-efficacy, and ultimately, increased intrinsic motivation to perform the task.

Recent cognitive rehabilitation work increasingly emphasizes motivation, self-efficacy, and task engagement

Data also suggest that, in schizophrenia, cognitive rehabilitation exerts its effects through top down mechanisms, such as helping people recruit the cognitive operations most appropriate for a given situation or task, as opposed to improvements in basic processes (Spaulding et al., 1999a, 1999b). This conclusion is consistent with data demonstrating that creating task conditions to facilitate top-down processing can improve performance even on basic visual processing tasks (Phillips & Silverstein, 2003; Silverstein et al., 1996). More recent treatment data (Reeder et al., 2004) suggest that cognitive rehabilitation improves functioning by increasing the extent to which a person adopts an organizational framework in which they respond to external feedback as opposed to internal cues. In analyzing the results from two randomized controlled trials of cognitive rehabilitation, Reeder et al. (2004) found that changes in verbal working memory were not related to changes in functional outcome, whereas an increased tendency to respond according to external feedback was associated with positive outcomes. This is relevant to attention shaping, where the primary goal of the intervention is to use structured, frequent, behavior (attentiveness)-linked, external feedback to motivate patients to attend to content being taught to them. In short, recent work in cognitive rehabilitation suggests that its effectiveness is a function of the extent to which variables such as motivation, self-efficacy and task-engagement are addressed.

4.2.1   Recovery-Oriented Perspectives

Little work has been done on consumer perspectives about the mechanisms involved in their recovery. However, a recent study (Roe, 2001) identified several themes that were frequent in patient narratives about their own change over time. One theme was the importance of the role and meaning of work. Work was viewed as a context to practice adjustment, a setting for providing social contacts, an avenue for generating a more functional sense of self (in contrast, not working reflected and reinforced a sense of shame, helplessness, and lack of agency), an activity that fostered a diminishment of symptoms, an activity that generated purpose and meaning in one's life, and that provided a source of money and material survival. A second theme involved expectations and attitudes toward treatment, especially a desire to eliminate symptoms, to gain an understanding and a sense of control over the illness, and to restore aspects of premorbid functioning. The third and fourth themes identified by patients as important to recovery were a desire for more relationships and the elimination of obstacles in establishing and maintaining satisfying relationships.

People with schizophrenia see work, positive expectations from treatment, and improved social relationships as being important to their recoveries

Self-esteem also appears to be an important factor involved in recovery. In a recent study, change in self-esteem between discharge and one-year follow-up significantly predicted scores on the Brief Psychiatric Rating Scale, the Global Assessment Scale, and the Strauss-Carpenter Outcome Scale (measuring frequency and quality of social relations, quality and quantity of work, duration of time outside hospital, and level of symptoms) (Roe, 2003). This led the author of that study to conclude that "Sustaining esteem despite the illness should become an important goal of treatment, and the impact of interventions on consumers' esteem should be considered and evaluated . . . An extremely passive, dependent, and compliant person receiving treatment who has low self-esteem and few symptoms may not necessarily have a better course of recovery than a more symptomatic treatment consumer who sustains hope, goals, sense of purpose, and self-esteem." (Roe, 2003).

The act of generating and sharing recovery stories/narratives is a critical, but neglected factor in the self-transformation process. Self-transformation signifies the creation of a new vision of who we believe we are. Recovery stories can be seen as a form of autobiographical narrative, or personal myth. Creating a personal myth involves creating a story about oneself as a temporal being that has a past, and relating the present to this past in order to form a perspective of the future (Popp-Baier, 2001). A decisive change in the life of the narrator is a key theme in such stories. For many schizophrenia patients, the adoption of a recovery perspective can be seen as such a decisive change. The reconstruction of one's life narrative has been previously noted as a mechanism operative in psychotherapy (Shaw, 2000), and the adoption of new religious beliefs (Silverstein, 1988).

The construction of recovery-oriented personal narratives can have a transformative effect

A key distinction in understanding the effects of generating new personal narratives is that between referential and constitutive speech acts. Referential speech refers to objects or events with shared meaning (e.g., "I have a headache" when trying to communicate a feeling of a pain in the head). Constitutive speech acquires meaning via the context in which it occurs, and often involves nonverbal behaviors (e.g., "I have a headache" to indicate to the person next to you that another person that is speaking is boring, or conveying one's political orientation by wearing buttons supportive of a particular candidate). In this way, engaging in discussion about one's recovery can be seen as an important component to the recovery process itself. This is because such speech acts, while referential in the sense of describing behaviors and feelings, are also constitutive in that they signify personal involvement in, and a deepening commitment to, the recovery process. Therefore, recovery-oriented discourse (ROD) becomes constitutive by establishing links between recovery concepts and individual experience. ROD becomes the new frame of reference from within which new ideas and feelings about the self can emerge and be enacted. A person becomes more deeply committed to recovery through the act of speaking about it. ROD enables verbal expression of previously inaccessible or unacceptable ideas/desires, while deepening the commitment to the recovery orientation. The recovery narrative constitutes the self-transformation of the narrator. The process of recovery is gradual, as recovery-oriented meanings are attributed to ongoing experiences. Meaning is not contained in a single event or set of events. Rather, performance or telling of the recovery-oriented narrative is an essential part of the process of self-transformation.

In addition to the importance of speaking the recovery-oriented narrative, the self-transformation will be dialogically sustained by interactions with others with similar views (including through peer-support and work with recovery-oriented mental health professionals). This is important because it has been suggested that people actualize narratives "not only by recounting them, but also by listening to them and recounting *themselves through them*; in other words, by putting them into 'play' in their institutions – thus by assigning themselves the posts of narratee and diegesis as well as the post of narrator" (Lyotard, 1984, p. 23).

4.3   Efficacy and Prognosis

Effectiveness and efficacy data on various psychological treatments for schizophrenia have been noted above in the review of specific interventions. In this section, we note and comment on the findings of recent reviews and practice guidelines regarding which interventions should be considered "best practices" or "evidence-based practices" for the treatment of schizophrenia.

The most comprehensive effort to date to review the treatment literature is that of the Patient Outcomes Research Team (PORT), which published a major review and set of recommendations in the late 1990s (Lehman et al., 1998), and then an update in 2004 (Lehman et al., 2004). In the PORT articles, psychological treatments are divided into several types of interventions, including psychotherapies, family interventions, vocational rehabilitation, and community-based interventions. Two recommendations were presented regarding individual and group therapy. The first was that therapies adhering to a psychodynamic model should not be used in the treatment of schizophrenia due to lack of evidence of their effectiveness and some evidence that they can be harmful. As noted above in the discussion of psychodynamic therapies, this is an oversimplified conclusion, although it is accurate in cases of acute psychosis and in other cases when administered by inexperienced therapists. With stable patients and experienced therapists, however, the data indicate that schizophrenia patients can benefit from this form of treatment. The second PORT recommendation about psycho-therapy was that treatments using "well-specified" combinations of support, education, and behavioral and cognitive skills training have demonstrated ef-fectiveness and should be used. This recommendation applies to multiple inter-ventions, all of which have demonstrated effectiveness in multiple studies. These include individual cognitive behavior therapy for psychotic symptoms, group-based skills training approaches, and psychoeducational approaches.

The PORT report highlighted studies demonstrating positive effects of family psychoeducation programs. The report noted that this intervention should not be restricted only to families with high levels of expressed emotion, and that the programs should be of at least 9 months duration. Several specific types of family psychoeducation were cited as being effective. It was also noted that family interventions that are based on the idea that family dysfunction causes schizophrenia should not be used.

Studies of supported employment have consistently demonstrated improved vocational outcomes compared to "train-place" programs. For example, in the Mueser et al. (2004) Hartford Supported Employment Study, the supported em-ployment group was superior to the psychosocial rehabilitation and "train-place" conditions on the following variables: days to first job (to PSR only); percentage in any competitive job (74% vs. 18% vs. 27.5%); percentage work-ing more than 20 hours per week; total hours worked; total wages earned; total weeks worked; average weeks per job; weeks at longest job; satisfaction with first job; and the percentage retaining a job after 2 years (> 90% vs. 40–50% vs. < 40%). While these and similar results are promising, much more remains to be done. In the Mueser et al. study cited above, for example, among patients in the supported employment group, only 33.8% of patients were working more than 20 hours per week, the average number of weeks worked out of a total of 104 (2 years) was 29.72, the average number of weeks at the longest job was 25.54, and the average amount earned over the two-year period was $2,078. In short, while supported employment programs are superior to older forms of vocational rehabilitation, few patients are as yet able to return to full-time work over the long-term, and to be paid significant wages.

Placing people in jobs of their choice in the community and provid-ing supports as needed leads to better voca-tional outcomes

The final area of psychosocial treatment recommended by the PORT report was assertive community treatment (ACT). A specific form of ACT, known as the Program for Assertive Community Treatment (PACT) (Stein & Test, 1980), includes standards and a model for community-based care that has demonstrat-ed effectiveness in past studies. Some of the effects associated with PACT in-clude reduction in hospital use, increased retention in mental health services, increase in housing stability, and a moderate improvement in symptoms and quality of life. PACT by itself does not appear to improve social functioning. As with many standardized interventions, the degree of fidelity to standards of the ACT program model is related to outcome. This is especially true for the factors of shared caseloads, patient to staff ratios near 10:1, 24-hour availability, having a nurse on the team, and daily team meetings. Two issues preventing a full assessment of the effectiveness of ACT are the lack of a consensus to date on the percentage of schizophrenia patients that should receive ACT, and esti-mates that only approximately 2% of patients are receiving such services (Leh-man & Steinwachs, 2003). ACT works best when embedded within a well-fi-nanced and managed service system, and the relative lack of such systems is a contributing factor to the low delivery rate.

A discussion of social learning programs was omitted from the PORT report, despite the evidence for their effectiveness being among the strongest of any treatment in the mental health field (Paul & Lentz, 1977; Paul & Menditto, 1992). The effectiveness of social learning programs is due to the strength of its component behavioral interventions, including skills training, behavior contracting, shaping, differential reinforcement, extinction, time-out procedures, token economy, and rigorous use of staff training and observational rating procedures (of both patients and staff).

Also not mentioned in the PORT report was cognitive rehabilitation. Since the publication of the initial PORT recommendations paper in 1998, however, many more studies on cognitive rehabilitation have been published. Moreover, effectiveness has been demonstrated for several models of treatment, including integrated psychological therapy (Spaulding et al., 1999a, 1999b), the neuropsychological-educational approach to remediation (NEAR) (Medalia et al., 2000), cognitive enhancement therapy (Hogarty et al., 2004), neurocognitive enhancement therapy (Wexler & Bell, 2005), attention shaping procedures (Silverstein et al., 2005a), errorless learning (Kern et al., 2005), cognitive remediation therapy (Wykes, et al., 2003), and cognitive adaptation training (Velligan, et al., 2002).

4.4   Variations and Combinations of Methods

Perhaps more than any other psychological or psychiatric disorder, treatment of schizophrenia and serious mental illness requires coordinated use of multiple modalities. This is partly due to the pervasive nature of serious mental illness, that is, the presence of impairments or other problems throughout the physiological, cognitive, behavioral and social levels of a person's functioning. Also, the concept of *recovery* as a desired outcome demands that treatment and rehabilitation address all aspects of the person's functioning, in order to achieve the best possible quality of life.

Unfortunately, our understanding of the treatment and rehabilitation of serious mental illness is somewhat fragmented. Development of psychopharmacological, psychological and social interventions has historically been undertaken in relative isolation, research on each being minimally informed by research on the others. Development of psychiatric rehabilitation encouraged "cross-talk" between areas of research, and this is accelerating with the promotion of the recovery concept. Nevertheless, systematic approaches to integrating and coordinating the many modalities of psychiatric rehabilitation have only recently begun to appear (e.g., Spaulding, Sullivan, & Poland, 2003).

The key to integrating and coordinating services for serious mental illness is in the organization and functioning of an *interdisciplinary treatment team* (Liberman, Hilty, Drake, & Tsang, 2001). The team consists of the person in recovery, legally appointed substitute decision makers where applicable (e.g., parents, guardian, or a mental health court), and the professionals and paraprofessionals who provide services. Ideally, it is the treatment team's collective responsibility to produce a *formulation* of the person in recovery's disabilities and other problems, and a *treatment plan*, a hypothesis-driven and data-driven strategy for treating or otherwise overcoming the problems.

Formal treatment plans are required by healthcare accreditation standards, such as those of the Joint Commission on Accreditation of Healthcare Organizations (JCAHO) and the Commission on Accreditation of Rehabilitation Facilities (CARF). It is therefore common to find treatment plans in hospitals and institutions that serve people with severe mental illness. However, use of case formulation, such as that exemplified by the multimodal functional model (MFM) is not required, and it is not common to find treatment plans systematically informed by that approach. As a result, treatment is not usually provided in a systematic, coordinated way. Hopefully, the national call for mental health reform will lead to more widespread use of modern rehabilitation and recovery-based approaches for serious mental illness, and this will lead to more uniform use of case formulation and integrated treatment.

Case management is another approach to managing the need for multiple treatments and other services. It is usually used in outpatient clinics or other community settings. A case manager collects assessments and recommendations from other practitioners, arranges or "brokers" needed services, and ensures that the services are provided. Case management does not necessarily include a treatment team that shares collective responsibility for rehabilitation and recovery, or an integrated formulation that guides treatment. Although case management is probably cost effective for people who have mild to moderate disabilities, it is generally considered ineffective for people with the most severe disabilities.

Assertive community treatment (ACT) is an upgrade of case management specially designed for people with severe disabilities. ACT was originally a translation of hospital-based treatment to community settings, and was in fact characterized as a "hospital without walls." Aspects of hospital practice adapted for community use in ACT included treatment teams with collective responsibility for all services, systematic treatment planning, 24-hour availability of practitioners and "assertive" intervention by practitioners whenever needed (i.e.,not requiring the initiative of the recipient),. Since ACT originally emulated medical model hospital practice, case formulation did not replace psychiatric diagnosis as the basis for guiding treatment. Since its origins, ACT has been hybridized with rehabilitation and recovery. As a result, both medical model and rehabilitation/recovery versions of ACT are in use today. Both versions of ACT have proven effective in preventing rehospitalization. However, not surprisingly, medical model ACT uninformed by rehabilitation and recovery concepts does not appear effective at helping people improve their personal and social functioning.

4.5   Problems in Carrying out the Treatment

There are numerous challenges and barriers to the implementation of evidence-based treatment and rehabilitation technologies for individuals with schizophrenia and related disorders. Many clinicians are not interested in working with such individuals and/or not adequately trained to implement effective services for them. Often they are prepared as general practitioners through their graduate training, and are not trained in more specific approaches to working with individuals with severe mental disorders. As a result, they attempt to apply the individual and/or group psychotherapies with which they are more familiar. Many of these treatments are more appropriate for individuals with less severe and complex disorders, and, as such, of limited effectiveness for people with schizophrenia. Contributing to this problem, is the typically nonexistent to limited focus in most graduate training programs on treatment and rehabilitation approaches for individuals with severe and complex mental disorders. It is incumbent upon graduate training programs in mental health disciplines to better address these issues and provide more training and clinical experience for students in the implementation of evidence-based practices in this area. A related barrier is the tendency of many clinicians to get most of their information about treatment from pharmaceutical company marketing materials (Bromley, 2005). This tendency leads to a failure to learn about effective psychological treatments.

Other barriers to the implementation of effective services for individuals with schizophrenia and related disorders pertain to the organizational systems in which services are delivered. Most people with such disorders receive services from state or federally funded public mental health facilities or nonprofit agencies that contract with states. Generally, these organizations have limited resources for the training and consultation often necessary for the implementation of innovative treatment technologies. The dissemination of advances in effective clinical interventions identified through research requires training for staff working in the field. Many of these new clinical interventions are quite sophisticated and cannot be learned through a brief workshop or two. They require ongoing training, consultation, and supervision. Many public mental health agencies are unable or unwilling to allocate the resources to support this level of training. Furthermore, many clinical innovations are systemic in nature and involve multiple service components delivered by different staff. This introduces a whole host of challenges associated with organizing many diverse staff of various disciplines and levels of expertise into a coherent service delivery system (Spaulding, Sullivan, & Poland, 2003; Stuve & Menditto, 1999). In addition to training and consultation, implementation of systemic changes requires organizational buy in and considerable administrative support. However, changing organizational cultures and rallying and maintaining the kind of administrative commitment necessary to move an organization in the direction of implementing evidence-based practices is often difficult, at best.

Nonetheless, despite the many challenges and barriers to implementing evidence-based services for individuals diagnosed with schizophrenia and related disorders, increasing pressures are mounting to require mental health service delivery systems to offer such services. The SAMHSA (2004) has developed a system for evaluating and listing evidence-based programs on its website. Additionally, SAMHSA has sponsored the development of a series of toolkits which are available at no charge on its website (http://www.mentalhealth.samhsa.gov/cmhs/communitysupport/toolkits/). The influential President's New Freedom Commission on Mental Health Report (President's New Freedom Commission on Mental Health, 2003) includes as one of its goals: "Advance evidence-based practices using dissemination and demonstration projects and create a public-private partnership to guide their implementation" (p. 80). These actions at the federal level inevitably will guide future funding directions and create increased expectations and accountability for mental health service delivery systems and agencies. As a result, perhaps now more than at any other time in history the atmosphere is ripe for widespread dissemination and adoption of evidence-based treatment and rehabilitation services for individuals with severe mental disorders.

5

Case Vignette

John is a 20-year-old male from a city in the eastern U. S. who developed auditory hallucinations and paranoid delusions during his junior year at a college on the west coast. After a period of increased marijuana use, declining concentration, increasing anxiety, social isolation, angry outbursts in public places (e.g., cafeteria), and, eventually, paranoid thinking and auditory hallucinations, he was hospitalized for three weeks, during which time he began taking risperidone. After leaving the hospital, he withdrew from his university, returned to his parents' home, and developed a treatment relationship with an outpatient psychiatrist. John's hallucinations and paranoia were significantly reduced although still present at times. His parents were encouraged by the reduction of inappropriate behavior, but gradually became concerned that John was not doing anything with his life. On a typical day he would sleep late, watch TV most of the day, not go out of the house, and then stay up late reading or smoking in his room. This led increasingly to interactions with his family in which they criticized him for being lazy and not "getting on with his life." The results of these stressful interactions were further withdrawal and increasing frustration on the part of his parents. In response to these issues, John's psychiatrist suggested that John meet with a psychologist for individual therapy and to help him move forward with his life. It was also suggested that the family go for family therapy, which they agreed to do. In a time-limited form of multiple family psychoeducation, John's family learned about schizophrenia, including about negative symptoms and the importance of not blaming the patient for them, and about effective communication and conflict resolution skills. This gradually improved the environment in the home. John also began meeting with a psychologist once (and sometimes twice) a week. The initial focus of these meetings was to clarify John's short-term goals, which included returning to school and living independently. John enrolled in a local college and began taking a full courseload, against the advice of his family and treatment providers. However, he soon found that his ability to focus on the lectures and readings was not at his premorbid level and he was occasionally distracted by hearing voices. He was therefore put in touch with supported education services at his school, and a counselor began working with him to promote study habits that would lead to maximum retention of information. He also eventually agreed to drop two of his courses. At this point, the focus of therapy shifted to a cognitive behavioral model, to help John cope better with his voices, and to reduce anxiety and paranoia by recognizing attributional errors and generating more appropriate thoughts about interpersonal situations. A continuing issue, however, was John's continued desire to use marijuana. During periods of increased workload, or when considering going to social events at school, he would smoke in order to feel relaxed, although he often developed unusual thoughts and paranoia instead. John recognized that he had a problem, and agreed to attend a 3 times per week dual-diagnosis group that used the UCLA Substance Abuse Management Module at a local mental health center. He received a great deal of social support from the group, as well as information about the adverse effects of marijuana on his psychiatric condition. John was eventually able to cut down his marijuana use significantly.

6

Further Reading

Bellack, A.S., Mueser, K.T., Gingerich, S., & Agresta, J. (1997). *Social skills training for schizophrenia: A step-by-step guide.* New York: Guilford. A user-friendly guide and set of materials for conducting an effective form of social skills training.

Chadwick, P., Birchwood, M., & Trower, P. (1996). *Cognitive therapy for delusions, voices, and paranoia.* New York: Wiley. An excellent introduction to CBT for psychosis, along with many helpful case examples, transcripts of therapist-client interactions, and discussion of conceptual issues.

Corrigan, P.W., & Liberman, R.P. (Eds.), *Behavior therapy in psychiatric hospitals.* New York: Springer Publishing Company. Full of useful information and data about behavioral treatment approaches for inpatient (including forensic) schizophrenia patients.

Davidson, L. (2003). *Living outside mental illness: qualitative studies of recovery in schizophrenia.* New York: New York University Press. Pioneering book about the experience of people with schizophrenia as they begin to move beyond seeing themselves as patients, and toward more meaningful identities.

Fuller-Torrey, E. (2001). *Surviving schizophrenia: A Manual for Families, Consumers, and Providers (4th Edition).* New York: Collins. An excellent resource about research findings on schizophrenia, and current treatment options.

Heinrichs, R.W. (2001). *In search of madness: Schizophrenia and neuroscience.* New York: Oxford University Press. An excellent summary of the research on neuropsychological and neuroscientific findings.

Liberman, R.P., DeRisi, W.J., & Mueser, K.T. (2001). *Social skills training for psychiatric patients.* Boston: Allyn & Bacon. Another user-friendly guide for conducting an effective form of social skills training.

Lieberman, J. (2001). *Comprehensive care of schizophrenia.* London: Taylor and Francis. A thorough review of current treatment options. Written primarily for clinicians but consumers and family members can learn from this as well.

Mueser, K.T., Noordsy, D.L., Drake, R.E., & Fox, L. (2003). *Integrated treatment for dual disorders: A guide to effective practice.* New York: Guilford. Comprehensive summary of all important treatment components involved in treating dually diagnosed clients, including discussions of assessment, individual, group, family, and residential approaches, and motivational interviewing, along with many useful handouts and tools.

Sadock, B.J., & Sadock, V.A. (Eds.). *Kaplan & Sadock's comprehensive textbook of psychiatry* (8th Ed.). New York: Lippincott, Williams, & Wilkins. Many excellent chapters on schizophrenia, covering a range of topics including conceptualization, diagnosis, treatment, cognitive and biological findings, etc.

Sass, L. (1992). *Madness and modernism.* Cambridge, MA: Harvard University Press. A fascinating description of the inner world of many schizophrenia patients, using insights drawn from phenomenological philosophy.

Whitaker, R. (2003). *Mad in America: Bad science, bad medicine, and the enduring mistreatment of the mentally ill.* Cambridge, MA: Perseus. A scathing indictment of the medical and pharmaceutical professions in terms of treatment of schizophrenia.

References

Abramowitz, I.A., & Coursey, R.D. (1989). Impact of an educational support group on family participants who take care of their schizophrenic relatives. *Journal of Consulting and Clinical Psychology, 57,* 232–236.

Allness, D., & Knoedler, W. (2003). *The PACT model of community-based treatment for persons with severe and persistent mental illnesses: A manual for PACT start-up.* Arlington, VA: National Alliance for the Mentally Ill.

American Psychiatric Association. (1994). *Diagnostic and statistical manual for mental disorders* (4th Ed.). Washington DC: Author.

Andreasen, N.C. (1984a). *The Scale for the Assessment of Negative Symptoms (SANS).* Iowa City, IA: The University of Iowa.

Andreasen, N.C. (1984b). *The Scale for the Assessment of Positive Symptoms (SANS).* Iowa City, IA: The University of Iowa.

Andreasen, N.C., Paradiso, S., & O'Leary, D.S. (1998). "Cognitive Dysmetria" as an integrative theory of schizophrenia: A dysfunction in cortical-subcortical-cerebellar circuitry? *Schizophrenia Bulletin, 24,* 203–218.

Andreasson, S., Allebeck, P., Engstrom, A., & Rydberg, U. (1987). Cannabis and schizophrenia: A longitudinal study of Swedish conscripts. *Lancet, 2*(8574), 1483–1486.

Anthony, W.A., Cohen, M., & Farkas, M. (1990). *Psychiatric rehabilitation.* Boston: Center for Psychiatric Rehabilitation.

Arseneault, L., Cannon, M., Poulton., R., Murray, R., Caspi, A., & Moffitt, T.E. (2002). Cannabis use in adolescence and risk for adult psychosis: longitudinal prospective study. *British Medical Journal, 325,* 1212–1213.

Attkisson, R.F., Crook, J., Karno, M., Lehman, A., McGlashan, T.H., Meltzer, H.Y. et al. (1992). Clinical services research. *Schizophrenia Bulletin, 18,* 561–626.

Bachmann, S., Resch, F., & Mundt, C. (2003). Psychological treatment for psychosis: history and overview. *Journal of the American Academy of Psychoanalysis and Dynamic Psychiatry, 31,* 155–176.

Baddeley, A.D. (1992). Implicit memory and errorless learning: A link between cognitive theory and neuropsychological rehabilitation? In L.R. Squire & N. Butters (Eds.) *Neuropsychology of memory* (2nd ed.) (pp. 309–314). New York: Guilford.

Baldwin, L., Beck, N., Menditto, A., Arms, T., & Cormier, J.F. (1992). Decreasing excessive water drinking by chronic mentally ill forensic patients. *Hospital and Community Psychiatry, 43,* 507–509

Barlow, D.H., & Hersen, M. (1984). *Single case experimental designs: Strategies for studying behavior change* (2nd ed.). New York: Pergamon.

Beas, M.I., & Salanova, M. (in press). Self-efficacy beliefs, computer training and psychological well being among information and communication technology workers. *Computers in Human Behavior.*

Beck, A.T. (1971). Cognitive patterns in dreams and daydreams. In J.H. Masserman (Ed.), *Dream dynamics* (pp. 2–7). New York: Grune & Stratton.

Beck, A.T., & Rector, N.A. (2005). Cognitive approaches to schizophrenia: Theory and therapy. *Annual Review of Clinical Psychology, 1,* 577–606.

Beck, N.C., Menditto, A.A., Baldwin, L., Angelone, E., & Maddox, M. (1991). Reduced frequency of aggressive behavior in forensic patients in a social learning program. *Hospital and Community Psychiatry, 42,* 750–752.

Bell, M., Bryson, G., & Wexler, B.E. (2003). Cognitive remediation of working memory deficits: Durability of training effects in severely impaired and less severely impaired schizophrenia. *Acta Psychiatrica Scandinavica, 108,* 101–109.

Bellack, A., Blanchard, J., Murphy, P., & Podell, K. (1996). Generalization effects of training on the Wisconsin Card Sorting Test for schizophrenia patients. *Schizophrenia Research, 19,* 189–194.

Bellack, A.S., Morrison, R.L., Mueser, K.T., Wade, J.H., & Sayers, S.L. (1990). Role play for assessing the social competence of psychiatric patients. *Psychological Assessment: A Journal of Consulting and Clinical Psychology, 2,* 248–255.

Bellack, A.S., Sayers, M., Mueser, K.T., & Bennet, M. (1994). An evaluation of social problem solving in schizophrenia. *Journal of Abnormal Psychology, 103,* 371–378.

Bellack, A.S., Schooler, N. R, Marder, S.R., Kane, J.M., Brown, C.H., & Yang, Y. (2004). Do clozapine and risperidone affect social competence and problem solving? *American Journal of Psychiatry, 161,* 364–367.

Bellus, S.B., Kost, P.P., Vergo, J.G., Gramse, R., & Weiss, B.A. (1999). Academic skills, self-care skills and on-ward behavior with cognitively impaired, chronic psychiatric inpatients. *Psychiatric Rehabilitation Skills, 3,* 23–40.

Bender, (1966). The concept of plasticity in childhood schizophrenia. *Proceedings of the Annual Meeting of the American Psychopathological Association, 54,* 354–365.

Benedict, R., Harris, A., Markow, T., McCormick, J., Nuechterlein, K., & Asarnow, R. (1994). Effects of training in information processing in schizophrenia. *Schizophrenia Bulletin, 20,* 537–546.

Benton, M., & Schroeder, H. (1990). Social skills training with schizophrenics: A meta-analytic evaluation. *Journal of Consulting and Clinical Psychology, 58,* 741–747.

Bleuler, E. (1950). *Dementia praecox or the group of schizophrenias.* New York: International Universities Press. [Originally published as *Dementia praecox oder die gruppe der schizophrenien,* 1911.]

Bleuler, M. (1978). *The schizophrenic disorders: Long-term patient and family studies* (S. M Clemens, trans.). New Haven, CT: Yale University Press.

Böker, W., & Brenner, H.D. (1983). Selbstheilungsversuche schizophrener. *Nervenarzt, 54,* 578–589.

Bond, G., Dincin, J., Setze, P., & Witheridge, T. (1984). The effectiveness of psychiatric rehabilitation: A summary of research at Thresholds. *Psychosocial Rehabilitation Journal, 7,* 6–22.

Brenner, H., Hodel, B., Roder, V., & Corrigan, P. (1992). Treatment of cognitive dysfunctions and behavioral deficits in schizophrenia. *Schizophrenia Bulletin, 18,* 21–26.

Brenner, H., Roder, V., Hodel, B., Kienzle, N., Reed, D., & Liberman, R: (1994). *Integrated psychological therapy for schizophrenic patients.* Toronto: Hogrefe & Huber.

Brieff, R. (1994). Personal computers in psychiatric rehabilitation: A new approach to skills training. *Hospital and Community Psychiatry, 45,* 207–260.

Broen, W.E. (1968). *Schizophrenia: Research and theory.* New York: Academic Press.

Broen, W.E. Jr., & Storms, L.H. (1966). Lawful disorganization: The process underlying a schizophrenic syndrome. *Psychological Review, 73,* 265–279.

Bromley, E. (2005). A collaborative approach to targeted treatment development for schizophrenia: A qualitative evaluation of the NIMH-MATRICS project. *Schizophrenia Bulletin, 31,* 954–961.

Brook, B.D. (1973). Crisis hostel: An alternative to psychiatric hospitalization for emergency patients. *Hospital and Community Psychiatry, 24,* 621–624.

Buchanan, R.W., & Carpenter, W.T. (2005). Schizophrenia and other psychotic disorders. In B.J. Sadock & V.A. Sadock (Eds.), *Kaplan & Sadock's comprehensive textbook of psychiatry* (8th Ed.) (pp. 1329–1345). New York: Lippincott, Williams, & Wilkins.

Budoff, M. (1987). Measures for assessing learning potential. In C.S. Lidz (Ed.), *Dynamic assessment* (pp. 173–195). New York: Guilford.

Burns, B.J., & Santos, A.B. (1995). Assertive community treatment: An update of randomized trials. *Psychiatric Services, 46,* 669–675.

Burns, T, Creed, F., Fahy, T., Thompson, S., Tyrer, P., & White, I. (1999). Intensive vs. standard case management for severe psychotic illness: A randomised trial. *Lancet, 353,* 2185–2189.

Burns, T., Fioritti, A., Holloway, F., Malm, U., & Rossler, W. (2001) Case management and assertive community treatment in Europe. *Psychiatric Services, 52,* 631–636.

Byford, S., Fiander, M., Torgerson, D.J., Barber, J.A., Thompson, S.G., Burns, et al. (2000) Cost-effectiveness of intensive v. standard case management for severe psychotic illness. *British Journal of Psychiatry, 176,* 537–543

Calev, A., Korin, Y., Kugelmass, S., & Lerer, B. (1987). Performance of chronic schizophrenics on matched word and design recall tasks. *Biological Psychiatry, 22,* 699–709.

Cantor-Graae, E., & Selten, J-P. (2005). Schizophrenia and migration: A meta-analysis and review. *American Journal of Psychiatry, 162,* 12–24.

Campos, D.T., & Gieser, M.T. (1985). The psychiatric emergency/crisis disposition and community networks. *Emergency Health Services Review, 3,* 117–128.

Carpenter, W.T., Bartko, J.J., Carpenter, C.L., & Strauss, J.S. (1976). Another view of schizophrenia subtypes: A report from the International Pilot Study of Schizophrenia. *Archives of General Psychiatry 33,* 508–516.

Carpenter, W. T, & Gold, J.M. (2002). Another view of therapy for cognition in schizophrenia. *Biological Psychiatry, 51,* 969–971.

Carr, V., & Wale, J. (1986). Schizophrenia: an information processing model. *Australian and New Zealand Journal of Psychiatry, 20,* 136–155.

Caspi, A., Moffitt, T.E., Cannon, M., McClay, J., Murray, R., Harrington, H., et al. (2005). Moderation of the effect of adolescent-onset cannabis use on adult psychosis by a functional polymorphism in the catechol-O-methyltransferase gene: Longitudinal evidence of a gene X environment interaction. *Biological Psychiatry, 57,* 1117–1127.

Chadwick, P., Birchwood, M., & Trower, P. (1996). *Cognitive therapy for delusions, voices, and paranoia.* New York: Wiley.

Ciompi, L. (1980). Catamnestic long-term study on the course of life and aging of schizophrenics. *Schizophrenia Bulletin, 6,* 606–618.

Cicerone, K.D., Dahlberg, C., Kalmar, K., Langenbahn, D.M., Malec, J.F., Berquist, et al. (2000). Evidence-based cognitive rehabilitation: Recommendations for clinical practice. *Archives of Physical Medicine and Rehabilitation, 81,* 1596–1615.

Cohen, J.D., Barch, D.M., Carter, C., & Servan-Schreiber, D. (1999). Context–processing deficits in schizophrenia: Converging evidence from three theoretically motivated cognitive tasks. *Journal of Abnormal Psychology, 108,* 120–133.

Cohen, J.D., & Servan-Schreiber, D. (1992). Context, cortex, and dopamine: A connectionist approach to behavior and biology in schizophrenia. *Psychological Review, 99,* 45–777.

Condray, R. (2005). Language disorder in schizophrenia as a developmental learning disorder. *Schizophrenia Research, 73,* 5–20.

Conley, R.R., & Kelly, D.L. (2001). Management of treatment resistance in schizophrenia. *Biological Psychiatry, 50,* 898–911

Copeland, M.E. (1999). *Wellness recovery action plan.* West Dummerston, VT: Peach Press.

Corrigan, P.W., & Liberman, R.P. (Eds.). (1994). *Behavior therapy in psychiatric hospitals.* New York: Springer Publishing Company.

Corrigan, P.W., & Penn, D.L. (1995). The effects of antipsychotic and antiparkinsonian medication on psychosocial skill learning. *Clinical Psychology Science and Practice, 2,* 251–262.

Danion, J.M., Rizzo, L., & Bruant, A. (1999). Functional mechanisms underlying impaired recognition memory and conscious awareness in patients with schizophrenia. *Archives of General Psychiatry, 56,* 639–644.

Davidson, L., Shahar, G., Stayner, D.A., Chinman, M.J., Rakfeldt, J., & Tebes, J.K. (2004). Supported socialization for people with psychiatric disabilities: Lessons from a randomized controlled trial. *Journal of Community Psychology, 32,* 453–477.

DeSisto, M., Harding, C.M., McCormick, R.V., Ashikaga, T., & Brooks, G.W. (1995a). The Maine and Vermont three-decade studies of serious mental illness. II. Longitudinal course comparisons. *British Journal of Psychiatry, 167,* 338–342.

DeSisto, M.J., Harding, C.M., McCormick, R.V., Ashikaga, T., & Brooks, G.W. (1995b). The Maine and Vermont three-decade studies of serious mental illness. I. Matched comparison of cross-sectional outcome. *British Journal of Psychiatry, 167,* 331–338.

Dickerson, F. (2004). Update on cognitive behavioral psychotherapy for schizophrenia: Review of recent studies. *Journal of Cognitive Psychotherapy: An International Quarterly, 18,* 189–205.

Docherty, N.M., Hawkins, K.A., Hoffman, R.E., Quinlan, D., Rakfeldt, J., & Sledge, W.H. (1996). Working memory, attention, and communication disturbances in schizophrenia. *Journal of Abnormal Psychology, 105,* 212–219.

Dolder, C.R., Lacro, J.P., Leckband, S., & Jeste, D.V. (2003). Interventions to improve antipsychotic medication adherence: review of recent literature. *Journal of Clinical Psychopharmacology, 23,* 389–399.

Doody, G.A., Johnstone, E.C., Sanderson, T.L., Owens, D.G., & Muir, W.J. (1998). "Pfropfschizophrenie" revisited: Schizophrenia in people with mild learning disability. *The British Journal of Psychiatry, 173,* 145–153.

Drake, R., & Bellack, A. (2005). Psychiatric rehabilitation. In B.J. Sadock & V.A. Sadock (Eds.), *Kaplan & Sadock's comprehensive textbook of psychiatry* (8th Ed.) (pp. 1476–1487). New York: Lippincott, Williams, & Wilkins.

Drake, R.E., Mercer-McFadden, C., Mueser, K.T., McHugo, G.J., & Bond, G.R. (1998). Review of integrated mental health and substance abuse treatment for patients with dual disorders. *Schizophrenia Bulletin, 24,* 589–608.

Drake, R.E., & Mueser, K.T. (2000). Psychosocial approaches to dual diagnosis. *Schizophrenia Bulletin, 26,* 105–118.

Drake, R.E., & Mueser, K.T. (2001). Managing comorbid schizophrenia and substance abuse. *Current Psychiatry Reports, 3,* 418–422.

Drake, R.E., & Sederer, L.I. (1986). The adverse effects of intensive treatment of chronic schizophrenia. *Comprehensive Psychiatry, 27,* 313–326.

Dumont, J., & Jones, K. (2001, February). Findings from a consumer/survivor defined alternative to psychiatric hospitalization. Paper presented at the National Association of State Mental Health Program Directors Research Institute Conference, February 13, 2001.

Durham, T. (1997). Work-related activity for people with long-term schizophrenia: A review of the literature. *British Journal of Occupational Therapy, 60,* 248–252.

D'Zurilla, T.J. (1986). *Problem-solving therapy: A social competence approach to clinical intervention.* New York: Springer-Verlag.

D'Zurilla, T.J. (1988). Problem-solving therapies. In K.S. Dobson (Ed.), *Handbook of cognitive-behavioral therapies* (pp. 85–135). New York: Guilford.

D'Zurrila, T.J., & Goldfried, M.R. (1971). Problem-solving and behavior modification. *Journal of Abnormal Psychology, 78,* 107–126.

Edwards, J., Maude, D., McGorry, P.D., Harrigan, S.M., & Cocks, J.T. (1998). Prolonged recovery in first-episode psychosis. *British Journal of Psychiatry (Suppl.), 172,* 107–116.

Fairweather, G., Sanders, D., Maynard, H., & Cressler, D. (1969). *Community life for the mentally ill: An alternative to institutional care.* Chicago: Aldine.

Falloon, I.R., & Pederson, J. (1985). Family management in the prevention of morbidity of schizophrenia: The adjustment of the family unit. *British Journal of Psychiatry, 147,* 156–163.

Felton, C.J., Stastny, P., Shern, D.L., Blanch, A., Donahue, S.A., Knight, E., & Brown, C. (1995). Consumers as peer specialists on intensive case management teams: Impact on client outcomes. *Psychiatric Services, 46,* 1037–1044.

Feeney, T.J., & Ylvisaker, M. (2003). Context-sensitive behavioral supports for young children with TBI: Short-term effects and long-term outcome. *Journal of Head Trauma Rehabilitation, 18,* 33–51.

Fish, B. (1987). Infant predictors of the longitudinal course of schizophrenic development. *Schizophrenia Bulletin, 13,* 395–409.

Fiszdon, J.M., & Bell, M.D. (2004). Remédiation cognitive et thérapie occupationnelle dans le traitement ambulatoire du patient souffrant de schizophrénie [Cognitive remediation and work therapy in the outpatient treatment of patients with schizophrenia]. *Santé Mentale au Quebec, 29,* 117–142.

Flesher, S. (1990). Cognitive habilitation in schizophrenia: A theoretical review and model of treatment. *Neuropsychology Review, 1,* 223–246.

Galanter, M. (1988). Zealous self-help groups as adjuncts to psychiatric treatment: A study of Recovery, Inc. *American Journal of Psychiatry, 145,* 1248–1253.

Gitlin, M., Nuechterlein, K., Subotnik, K.L., Ventura, J., Mintz, J., Fogelson, D.L., Bartzokis, G., & Aravagiri, M. (2001). Clinical outcome following neuroleptic discontinuation in patients with remitted recent-onset schizophrenia. *American Journal of Psychiatry, 158,* 1835–1842.

Glass, L.L., Katz, H.M., Schnitzer, R.D., Knapp, P.H., Frank, A.F., & Gunderson, J.G. (1989). Psychotherapy of schizophrenia: An empirical investigation of the relationship of process to outcome. *American Journal of Psychiatry, 146,* 603–608.

Gold, J.M., Queern, C., Iannone, V.N., & Buchanan, R.W. (1999). Repeatable battery for the assessment of neuropsychological status as a screening test in schizophrenia I: Sensitivity, reliability, and validity. *American Journal of Psychiatry, 156,* 1944–1950.

Goldberg, T.E., Weinberger, D.R., Berman, K.F., Pliskin, N.H., & Podd, M.H. (1987). Further evidence for dementia of the prefrontal type in schizophrenia? A controlled study of teaching the Wisconsin Card Sorting Test. *Archives of General Psychiatry, 44,* 1008–1014.

Gordon, E., Cooper, N., Rennie, C., Hermens, D., & Williams, L.M. (2005). Integrative neuroscience: The role of a standardized database. *Clinical EEG and Neuroscience, 36,* 64–75.

Green, M.F. (1996). What are the functional consequences of cognitive deficits in schizophrenia? *American Journal of Psychiatry, 153,* 321–330.

Green, M.F. (1998). *Schizophrenia from a neurocognitive perspective.* Boston: Allyn & Bacon.

Green, M.F., Kern, R.F., Braff, D.L., & Mintz, J. (2000). Neurocognitive deficits and functional outcome: Are we measuring the "right stuff." *Schizophrenia Bulletin, 26,* 119–136.

Green, M.F., Nuechterlein, K.H., Gold, J.M., Barch, D.M., Cohen, J., Essock, S., et al. (2004). Approaching a consensus cognitive battery for clinical trials in schizophrenia: The NIMH-MATRICS conference to select cognitive domains and test criteria. *Biological Psychiatry, 56,* 301–307.

Green, M.F., Olivier, B., Crawley, J., Penn, D., & Silverstein, S. (2005). Social cognition in schizophrenia: Recommendations from the MATRICS New Approaches Conference. *Schizophrenia Bulletin, 31,* 882–887.

Gunderson, J.G., Frank, A.F., Katz, H.M., Vannicelli, M.L., Frosch, J.P., & Knapp, P.H. (1984). Effects of psychotherapy on schizophrenia: II. Comparative outcome of two forms of treatment. *Schizophrenia Bulletin, 10,* 564–598.

Haddock, G., Sellwood, W., Tarrier, N., & Yusupoff, L. (1994). Developments in cognitive-behavior therapy for persistent psychotic symptoms. *Behavior Change, 11,* 200–212.

Hall, J.A., Horgan, T.G., Stein, T.S., & Roter, D.L. (2002). Liking in the physician-patient relationship. *Patient Education and Counseling, 48,* 69–77.

Harding, C.M., Brooks, G.W., Ashikaga, T., Strauss, J.S., & Breier, A. (1987). The Vermont longitudinal study of persons with severe mental illness, II: Long-term outcome of subjects who retrospectively met DSM-III criteria for schizophrenia. *American Journal of Psychiatry, 144,* 727–735.

Hauff, E., Varvin, S., Laake, P., Melle, I., Vaglum, P., & Friis, S. (2002). Inpatient psychotherapy compared with usual care for patients who have schizophrenic psychoses. *Psychiatric Services, 53,* 471–473.

Harvey, P.D., Green, M.F., McGurk, S.R., & Meltzer, H.Y. (2003b). Changes in cognitive functioning with risperidone and olanzapine treatment: A large-scale, double-blind randomized study. *Psychopharmacology, 169,* 404–411.

Harvey, P.D., & Keefe, R.S.E. (2001). Studies of cognitive change in patients with schizophrenia following novel antipsychotic treatment. *American Journal of Psychiatry, 158,* 176–184.

Hatashita-Wong, M., & Silverstein, S.M. (2003). Coping with voices: selective attention training for persistent auditory hallucinations in treatment refractory schizophrenia. *Psychiatry, 66,* 255–261.

Heaton-Ward, A. (1977). Psychosis in mental handicap. *British Journal of Psychiatry, 130,* 525–533.

Heinssen, R.K. (2002). Improving medication compliance of a patient with schizophrenia through collaborative behavioral therapy. *Psychiatric Services, 53,* 255–257.

Heinssen, R.K., Liberman, R.P., & Kopelowicz, A. (2000). Psychosocial skills training for schizophrenia: Lessons from the laboratory. *Schizophrenia Bulletin, 26,* 21–46.

Henquet, C., Murray, R., Linszen, D., & van Os, J. (2005). The environment and schizophrenia: The role of cannabis use. *Schizophrenia Bulletin, 31,* 608–612.

Herz, M.I., Glazer, W.M., Mostert, M.A., Sheard, M.A., Szymanski, H.V., Hafez, H., Mirza, M., & Vana, J. (1991). Intermittent vs maintenance medication in schizophrenia. Two-year results. *Archives of General Psychiatry, 48,* 333–339.

Hobart, M.P., Goldberg, R., Bartko, J.J., & Gold, J.M. (1999). Repeatable battery for the assessment of neuropsychological status as a screening test in schizophrenia, II: convergent/discriminant validity and diagnostic group comparisons. *American Journal of Psychiatry, 156,* 1951–1957.

Hogarty, G. (2003) *Personal therapy for schizophrenia and related disorders: A guide to individualized treatment.* New York: Guilford.

Hogarty, G.E., & Flesher, S. (1999a). Developmental theory for a cognitive enhancement therapy of schizophrenia. *Schizophrenia Bulletin, 25,* 677–692.

Hogarty, G.E., & Flesher, S. (1999b). Practice principles of cognitive enhancement therapy for schizophrenia. *Schizophrenia Bulletin, 25,* 693–708.

Hogarty, G.E., Flesher, S., Ulrich, R., Carter, M., Greenwald, D., Pogue-Geile, M., Keshavan, M., Cooley, S., DiBarry, A.L., Garrett, A., Parepally, H., & Zoretich, R. (2004). Cognitive enhancement therapy for schizophrenia: Effects of a 2-year randomized trial on cognition and behavior. *Archives of General Psychiatry, 61,* 866–876.

Hogarty, G.E., Greenwald, D., Ulrich, R.F., Kornblith, S.J., DiBarry, A.L., Cooley, S., Carter, M., & Flesher, S. (1997). Three-year trials of personal therapy among schizophrenic patients living with or independent of family, II: Effects on adjustment of patients. *American Journal of Psychiatry, 154,* 1514–1524.

Holmes, E.P., Corrigan, P.W., Knight, P.W., & Flaxman, J. (1995). Development of a sleep management program for people with severe mental illness. *Psychiatric Rehabilitation Journal, 19,* 9–15.

Huber, G., Gross, G., & Schuttler, R. (1975). A long-term follow-up study of schizophrenia: psychiatric course of illness and prognosis. *Acta Psychiatrica Scandinavica, 52,* 49–57.

Huber, G., Gross, G., Schuttler, R., & Linz, M. (1980). Longitudinal studies of schizophrenic patients. *Schizophrenia Bulletin, 6,* 592–605.

IAPSRS: International Association of Psychosocial Rehabilitation Services. (1997). *Practice guidelines for the psychiatric rehabilitation of persons with severe and persistent mental illness in a managed care environment.* Columbia, MD: IAPSRS.

Ikebuchi, E., & Anzai, N. (1995). Effect of the medication management module evaluated using the role play test. *Psychiatry and Clinical Neuroscience, 49,* 151–156.

Jablensky, A., Sartorius, N., Ernberg, G., Anker, M., Korten, A., Cooper, et al. (1992). Schizophrenia: manifestations, incidence and course in different cultures. A World Health Organization ten-country study. *Psychological Medicine Monograph Supplement, 20,* 1–97.

Javitt, D.C., & Zukin, S.R. (1991). Recent advances in the phencyclidine model of schizophrenia. *American Journal of Psychiatry, 148,* 1301–1308.

Jones, N.T., Menditto, A.A., Geeson, L.R., Larson, E., & Sadewhite, L. (2001). Teaching social-learning procedures to paraprofessionals working with severely mentally-ill individuals in a maximum-security forensic hospital. *Behavioral Interventions, 16,* 167–179.

Kane, J.M., & Marder, S.R. (1993). Psychopharmacologic treatment of schizophrenia. *Schizophrenia Bulletin, 19,* 287–302.

Karon, B.P., & VandenBos, G.R. (1981). *Psychotherapy of schizophrenia. The treatment of choice.* New York: Jason Aronson.

Kavanagh, D.J., McGrath, J., Saunders, J.B., Dore, G., & Clark, D. (2002). Substance misuse in patients with schizophrenia: Epidemiology and management. *Drugs, 62,* 743–755.

Kay, S.R., Opler, L.A., & Fiszbein, A. (1987). The Positive and Negative Syndrome Scale (PANSS) for schizophrenia. *Schizophrenia Bulletin, 13,* 261–276.

Keefe, R.S., Goldberg, T.E., Harvey, P.D., Gold, J.M., Poe, M.P., & Coughenour, L. (2004). The Brief Assessment of Cognition in Schizophrenia: reliability, sensitivity, and comparison with a standard neurocognitive battery. *Schizophrenia Research, 68,* 283–297.

Keri, S., Kiss, I., Kelemen, O., Benedek, G., & Janka, Z. (2005). Anomalous visual experiences, negative symptoms, perceptual organization and the magnocellular pathway in schizophrenia: A shared construct? *Psychological Medicine, 35,* 1445–1455.

Kern, R.S. (1996). Cognitive rehabilitation of people with mental illness. *Psychiatric Rehabilitation Skills, 1,* 69–77.

Kern, R.S., Green, M.F., Goldstein, M.J. (1995). Modification of performance on the span of apprehension, a putative marker of vulnerability to schizophrenia. *Journal of Abnormal Psychology, 104,* 385–389.

Kern, R.S., Green, M.F., Mintz, J., & Liberman, R.P. (2003). Does "errorless learning" compensate for neurocognitive impairments in the work rehabilitation of persons with schizophrenia? *Psychological Medicine, 33,* 433–442.

Kern, R.S., Green, M.F., Mitchell, S., Kopelowicz, A., Mintz, J., & Liberman, R.P. (2005). Extensions of errorless learning for social problem-solving deficits in schizophrenia. *American Journal of Psychiatry, 162,* 513–519.

Kern, R.S., Liberman, R.P., Kopelowicz, A., Mintz, J., & Green, M.F. (2002). Applications of errorless learning for improving work performance in persons with schizophrenia. *American Journal of Psychiatry, 159,* 1921–1926.

Kern, R.S., Wallace, C.J., Hellman, S.G., Womack, L.M., & Green, M.F. (1996). A training procedure for remediating WCST deficits in chronic psychotic patients: An adaptation of errorless learning principles. *Journal of Psychiatric Research, 30,* 283–294. Erratum in: *Journal of Psychiatric Research, 31,* 1 (1997).

Kirkpatrick, B., Buchanan, R.W., Ross, D.E., & Carpenter, W.T., Jr. (2001). A separate disease within the syndrome of schizophrenia. *Archives of General Psychiatry, 58,* 165–171.

Kirkpatrick, B., & Tek, C. (2005). Schizophrenia: Clinical features and psychopathology concepts. In B.J. Saddock & V.A. Sadock (Eds.), *Kaplan & Sadock's comprehensive textbook of psychiatry* (8th ed.) (pp. 1416–1436). New York: Lippincott, Williams, & Wilkins.

Kissling, W. (1992). Ideal and reality of neuroleptic relapse prevention. *British Journal of Psychiatry Suppl(18),* 133–139.

Knight, R.A., & Silverstein, S.M. (1998). The role of cognitive psychology in guiding research on cognitive deficits in schizophrenia. In M.F. Lenzenweger & R.H. Dworkin (Eds.), *Origins and development of schizophrenia: Advances In experimental psychopathology* (pp. 247–295). Washington DC: APA Press.

Kopelowicz, A., & Liberman, R.P. (1995). Biobehavioral treatment and rehabilitation of schizophrenia. *Harvard Review of Psychiatry, 3,* 55–64.

Kopelowicz, A., Wallace, C.J., & Zarate, R. (1998). Teaching psychiatric inpatients to re-enter the community: A brief method of improving the continuity of care. *Psychiatric Services, 49,* 1313–1316.

Kraepelin, E. (1907). *Textbook of psychiatry* (7th ed.) (A.R. Diefendorf, Trans.). London: Macmillan.

Lam, D. (1991). Psychosocial family intervention in schizophrenia: A review of empirical studies. *Psychological Medicine, 21,* 423–441

Lecomte, T., Cyr, M., Lesage, A.D., Wilde, J., Leclerc, C., & Ricard, N. (1999). Efficacy of a self-esteem module in the empowerment of individuals with schizophrenia. *Journal of Nervous and Mental Disease, 187,* 406–413.

LePage, J.P. (1999). The impact of a token economy on injuries and negative events on an acute inpatient unit. *Psychiatric Services, 50,* 941–944.

Lehman, A.F., Kreyenbuhl, J., Buchanan, R.W., Dickerson, F.B., Dixon, L.B., Goldberg, R., et al. (2004). The Schizophrenia Patient Outcomes Research Team (PORT): Updated treatment recommendations 2003. *Schizophrenia Bulletin, 30,* 193–217.

Lehman, A.F., Steinwachs, D.S., and the Survey coinvestigators of the PORT Project (1998). Translating research into practice: the schizophrenia patient outcomes research team (PORT) treatment recommendations. *Schizophrenia Bulletin, 24,* 1–10.

Lehman, A.F., & Steinwachs, D.M. (2003). Evidence-based psychosocial treatment practices in schizophrenia: Lessons from the Patient Outcomes Research Team (PORT) project. *Journal of the American Academy of Psychoanalysis and Dynamic Psychiatry, 31,* 141–154.

Lehman, A.F., Ward, N.C., & Linn, L.S. (1982). Chronic mental patients: The quality of life issue. *American Journal of Psychiatry, 139,* 1271–1276.

Liberman, R.P. (Ed.). (1992). *Handbook of psychiatric rehabilitation.* Boston: Allyn & Bacon.

Liberman, R.P., & Corrigan, P.W. (1993). Designing new psychosocial treatments for schizophrenia. *Psychiatry, 56,* 238–249.

Liberman, R.P., Hilty, D.M., Drake, R.E., & Tsang, H.W. (2001). Requirements for multidisciplinary teamwork in psychiatric rehabilitation. *Psychiatric Services, 52,* 1331–1342.

Liberman, R.P., Kopelowicz, A., & Silverstein, S.M. (2005). Psychiatric rehabilitation. In B.J. Sadock & V.A. Sadock (Eds.), *Kaplan & Sadock's comprehensive textbook of psychiatry,* (8th ed.) (pp. 3884–3930). New York: Lippincott, Williams, & Wilkins.

Liberman, R.P., Kuehnel, T.G., & Backet, T.E. (1998). *Professional competencies for psychiatric rehabilitation.* Camarillo, CA: Psychiatric Rehabilitation Consultants.

Lieberman, J.A., Stroup, T.S., McEvoy, J.P., Swartz, M.S., Rosenheck, R.A., Perkins, D.O., Keefe, R.S., Davis, S.M., Davis, C.E., Lebowitz, B.D., Severe, J., Hsiao, J.K.; Clinical Antipsychotic Trials of Intervention Effectiveness (CATIE) Investigators. (2005). Effectiveness of antipsychotic drugs in patients with chronic schizophrenia. *New England Journal of Medicine, 353,* 1209–1223.

Lipton, F.R., Siegel, C., Hannigan, A., Samuels, J., & Baker, S. (2000). Tenure in supportive housing for homeless persons with severe mental illness. *Psychiatric Services, 51,* 479–486.

Llorents, S., Dschaufeli, W., Bakker, & Salanova, M. (in press). Does a positive gain spiral of resources, efficacy beliefs, and engagement exist? *Computers in Human Behavior.*

Loebel, A.D., Lieberman, J.A., Alvir, J.M., Mayerhoff, D.I., Geisler, S.H., & Szymanski, S.R. (1992). Duration of psychosis and outcome in first-episode schizophrenia. *American Journal of Psychiatry, 149,* 1183–1188.

Luke, D., Roberts, L, & Rappaport, J. (1994). Individual, group context, and individual-group fit predictors of self-help group attendance. In T.J. Powell (Ed), *Understanding the self-help organization: Frameworks and findings* (pp. 88–114). Thousand Oaks, CA: Sage.

Lyotard, J.F. (1984). *The post-modern condition: A report on knowledge* (G. Bennington & B. Massumi, Trans.). Minneapolis: University of Minnesota Press.

Lysaker, P.H., & Lysaker, J.T. (2002). Narrative structure in psychosis. *Theory and Psychology, 12,* 207–220.

Lysaker, P.H., & Lysaker, J.T. (2004). Schizophrenia as dialogue at the ends of its tether: The relationship of disruptions in identity with positive and negative symptoms. *Journal of Constructivist Psychology, 17,* 105–119.

Mace, F.C., Mauro, B.C., Boyajian, A.E., & Eckert, T.L. (1997). Effects of reinforcer quality on behavioral momentum: Coordinated applied and basic research. *Journal of Applied Behavior Analysis, 30,* 1–20.

MacDonald, A.W. III, Carter, C.S., Kerns, J.G., Ursu, S., Barch, D.M., Holmes, A.J., Stenger, V.A., & Cohen, J.D. (2005). Specificity of prefrontal dysfunction and context processing deficits to schizophrenia in never-medicated patients with first-episode psychosis. *American Journal of Psychiatry, 162,* 475–484.

MacKain, S., Smith, T., Wallace, C., & Kopelowicz, A. (1998). Evaluation of a community re-entry program. *International Review of Psychiatry, 10,* 76–83.

Martin, B.C., & Miller, L.S. (1998). Expenditures for treating schizophrenia: A population-based study of Georgia Medicaid recipients. *Schizophrenia Bulletin, 24,* 479–488.

Maslin, J. (2003). Substance misuse in psychosis: Contextual issues. In H.L. Graham, A. Copello, M.J. Birchwood, & K.T. Mueser (Eds.), *Substance misuse in psychosis: Approaches to treatment and service delivery* (pp. 3–23). West Sussex, England: Wiley,

McCreadie, R.G. and the Scottish Comorbidity Study Group. (2002). Use of drugs, alcohol, and tobacco by people with schizophrenia: Case-control study. *British Journal of Psychiatry, 181,* 321.

McFarlane, W., Link, B., Dushay, R., Marchal, J., & Crilly, J. (1995). Psychoeducational multiple family groups: Four-year relapse outcome in schizophrenia. *Family Process, 34,* 127–144.

McFarlane, W., Lukens, E., Link, B., Dushay, R., Deakins, S.A., & Newmark, M. (1995). Multiple-family groups and psychoeducation in the treatment of schizophrenia. *Archives of General Psychiatry, 52,* 79–687.

Medalia, A., Aluma, M., Tyron, W., & Merriam, A.E. (1998). Effectiveness of attention training in schizophrenia. *Schizophrenia Bulletin, 24,* 147–152.

Medalia, A., Dorn, H., & Watras-Gans, S. (2000). Treating problem solving deficits on an acute care psychiatric inpatient unit. *Psychiatry Research, 97,* 79–88.

Medalia A., Revheim, N., & Casey M. (2001). The remediation of problem-solving skills in schizophrenia. *Schizophrenia Bulletin, 27,* 259–267.

Medalia, A., & Revheim, N. (1998). Computer assisted learning in psychiatric rehabilitation. *Psychiatric Rehabilitation Skills, 3,* 77–98.

Medalia, A., Revheim, N., & Casey, M. (2000). Remediation of memory disorders in schizophrenia. *Psychological Medicine, 30,* 1451–1459.

Mednick, S.A., Huttunen, M.O., & Machon, R.A. (1994). Prenatal influenza infections and adult schizophrenia. *Schizophrenia Bulletin, 20,* 263–267.

Meichenbaum, D. (1969). The effects of instructions and reinforcement on thinking and language behavior of schizophrenics. *Behavior Research and Therapy, 7,* 101–114.

Meichenbaum, D.M., & Cameron, R. (1973). Training schizophrenics to talk to themselves: A means of developing attentional controls. *Behavior Therapy, 4,* 515–534.

Meltzer, H.Y., & McGurk, S.R. (1999). The effects of clozapine, risperidone, and olanzapine on cognitive function in schizophrenia. *Schizophrenia Bulletin, 25,* 233–255.

Menditto, A.A. (2002). A social-learning approach to the rehabilitation of individuals with severe mental disorders who reside in forensic facilities. *Psychiatric Rehabilitation Skills, 6,* 73–93.

Menditto, A.A., Baldwin, L.J., O'Neal, L.G., & Beck, N.C. (1991). Social learning procedures for increasing attention and improving basic skills in severely regressed institutionalized patients. *Journal of Behavior Therapy and Experimental Psychiatry, 22,* 265–269.

Menditto, A.A., Beck, N.C., Stuve, P., Fisher, J.A., Stacy, M., Logue, M.B., & Baldwin, L.J. (1996). Effectiveness of clozapine and a social learning program for severely disabled psychiatric inpatients. *Psychiatric Services, 47,* 46–51.

Menditto, A.A., Valdes, L., & Beck, N.C. (1994). Implementing a comprehensive social-learning program within the forensic psychiatric service of Fulton State Hospital. In P.W. Corrigan & R.P. Liberman (Eds.), *Behavior therapy in psychiatric hospitals.* New York: Springer-Verlag.

Menditto, A.A., Wallace, C.J., Liberman, R.P., Vander Wal, J., Jones, N.T., & Stuve, P. (1999). Functional assessment of independent living skills. *Psychiatric Rehabilitation Skills, 3,* 200–219.

Michie, A., Lindsay, W., & Smith, A. (1998). Changes following community living skills training: A controlled study. *British Journal of Clinical Psychology, 37,* 109–111.

Mojtabai, R., Nicholson, R.A., Isohanni, M., Jones, P., & Partennen, U. (1998). Role of psychosocial treatments in management of schizophrenia: A meta-analytic review of controlled outcome studies. *Schizophrenia Bulletin, 24,* 569–587.

Monroe-DeVita, M., & Mohatt, D. (1999). The state hospital and the community: An essential continuum for persons with severe and persistent mental illness. In W. Spaulding (Ed.), *The role of the state hospital in the 21st century: Vol. 84* (pp. 85–98). San Francisco: Jossey-Bass.

Morice, R., & Delehunty, A. (1996). Frontal/executive impairments in schizophrenia. *Schizophrenia Bulletin, 22,* 125–137.

Mosher, L. (1999). Soteria and other alternatives to acute psychiatric hospitalization: A personal and professional review. *Journal of Nervous and Mental Disease, 187,* 142–149.

Mosher, L.R., & Bola, J.R. (2000). The Soteria Project: Twenty-five years of swimming upriver. *Complexity and Change, 9,* 68–74.

Mosher, L.R., & Menn, A.Z. (1978). Community residential treatment for schizophrenia: Two-year follow-up. *Hospital and Community Psychiatry, 29,* 715–723.

Mueser, K., Bond, G., Drake, R., & Resnick, S. (1998). Models of community care for severe mental illness: A review of research on case management. *Schizophrenia Bulletin, 24,* 37–73.

Mueser, K.T., Clark, R.E., Haines, M., Drake, R.E., McHugo, G.J., Bond, G.R., et al. (2004). The Hartford study of supported employment for persons with severe mental illness. *Journal of Consulting and Clinical Psychology, 72,* 479–490.

Mueser, K.T., Corrigan, P.W., Hilton, D.W., Tanzman, B., Schaub, A., Gingerich, S., et al. (2002). Illness management and recovery: a review of the research. *Psychiatric Services, 53,* 1272–1284.

Nasrallah, H.A., & Smeltzer, D.J. (2003). *Contemporary diagnosis and management of the patient with schizophrenia.* Newtown, PA: Handbooks in Health Care.

Nuechterlein, K.H. (1991). Vigilance in schizophrenia and related disorders. In S.R. Steinhauer, J.H. Gruzelier, & J. Zubin (Eds.), *Handbook of schizophrenia: Neuropsychology, psychophysiology, and information processing. Vol. 5* (pp. 397–433). Amsterdam: Elsevier.

O'Brien, W.H., & Haynes, S.N. (1993). Behavioral assessment in the psychiatric setting. In A.S. Bellack & M. Hersen (Eds.), *Handbook of behavior therapy in the psychiatric setting* (pp. 39–71). New York: Plenum.

O'Carroll, R.E., Russell, H.H., Lawrie, S.M., & Johnstone, E.C. (1999). Errorless learning and the cognitive rehabilitation of memory-impaired schizophrenic patients. *Psychological Medicine, 29,* 105–112.

Olney, J.W., & Farber, N.B. (1995). Glutamate receptor dysfunction and schizophrenia. *Archives of General Psychiatry, 52,* 998–1007.

Palmer, B.W., Heaton, R.K., Paulsen, J.S., Kuck, J., Braff, D., Harris, et al. (1997). Is it possible to be schizophrenic yet neuropsychologically normal? *Neuropsychology, 11,* 437–446.

Park, S., & Holzman, P.S. (1992). Schizophrenics show spatial working memory deficits. *Archives of General Psychiatry, 49,* 975–981.

Parson, J., May, J., & Menoslascino, F.J. (1984). The nature and incidence of mental illness in mentally retarded individuals. In F.J. Menolascino & J.A. Stark (Eds.), *Handbook of mental illness in the mentally retarded.* New York. Plenum.

Patterson, T.L., Goldman, S., McKibbin, C.L., Hughs, T., & Jeste, D.V. (2001). UCSD Performance-Based Skills Assessment: Development of a new measure of everyday functioning for severely mentally ill adults. *Schizophrenia Bulletin, 27,* 235–245.

Paul, G.L. (1984). Residential treatment programs and after care for the chronically institutionalized. In M. Mirabi (Ed.), *The chronically mentally ill: Research and services.* New York: S.P. Medical & Scientific Books.

Paul, G.L. (Ed.). (1986). *Principles and methods to support cost-effective quality operations: Assessment in residential treatment settings (Part 1).* Champaign, IL: Research Press.

Paul, G.L. (Ed.). (1987). *Observational assessment instrumentation for service and research: The Time-Sample Behavioral Checklist for assessment in residential settings (Part 2).* Champaign, IL: Research Press.

Paul, G.L. (Ed.). (1988). *Observational assessment instrumentation for service and research: The Staff-Resident Interaction Chronograph: Assessment in residential treatment settings (Part 3).* Champaign, IL: Research Press.

Paul, G.L., & Lentz, R.J. (1977). *Psychosocial treatment of chronic mental patients: Milieu vs. social learning programs.* Cambridge, MA: Harvard University Press.

Paul, G.L., & Lentz, R.J. (1997). *Psychosocial treatment of chronic mental patients: Milieu vs. social learning programs (2nd ed.).* Cambridge, MA: Harvard University Press.

Paul, G.L., & Menditto, A.A. (1992). Effectiveness of inpatient treatment programs for mentally ill adults in public psychiatric facilities. *Applied and Preventive Psychology, 1,* 41–63.

Paul, G.L., Stuve, P., & Menditto, A.A. (1997). Social-learning program (with token economy) for adult psychiatric inpatients. *The Clinical Psychologist, 50,* 14–17.

Paul, R.H., Lawrence, J., Williams, L.M., Richard, C.C., Cooper, N., & Gordon, E. (2005). Preliminary validity of "integneuro": a new computerized battery of neurocognitive tests. *International Journal of Neuroscience, 115,* 1549–1567.

Pedersen, C.B., & Mortensen, P.B. (2001). Evidence of a dose-response relationship between urbanicity during upbringing and schizophrenia. *Archives of General Psychiatry, 58,* 1039–1046.

Phillips, W.A., & Silverstein, S.M. (2003). Impaired cognitive coordination in schizophrenia: Convergence of neurobiological and psychological perspectives. *Behavioral and Brain Sciences 23,* 65–138.

Phillips, W.A., & Singer, W. (1997). In search of common foundations for cortical computation. *Behavioral and Brain Sciences, 20,* 657–683.

Pilling, S., Bebbington, P., Kuipers, E., Garety, P., Geddes, J., Orbach, G., & Morgan, C. (2002). Psychological treatments in schizophrenia: I. Meta-analysis of family intervention and cognitive behaviour therapy. *Psychological Medicine, 32,* 763–782.

Policy Study Associates. (1989). *Best practice study of vocational rehabilitation services to severely mentally ill persons.* Washington, DC: Rehabilitation Services Administration, Department of Education.

Popp-Baier, U. (2001, September). Narrating Embodied Aims. Self-transformation in Conversion Narratives – A Psychological Analysis. *Forum Qualitative Sozialforschung / Forum: Qualitative Social Research [On-line Journal], 2(3).* Available at: http://www.qualitative-research.net/fqs-texte/3–01/3–01popp-e.htm.

Posner, C.M., Wilson, K.G., Kral, M.J., Lander, S., & McIlwraith, R.D. (1992). Family psychoeducational support groups in schizophrenia. *American Journal of Orthopsychiatry, 62,* 206–218.

Powell, T., Hill, E., Warner, L., Yeaton, W., & Silk, K. (2000). Encouraging people with mood disorders to attend a self-help group. *Journal of Applied Social Psychology, 30,* 2270–2288.

President's New Freedom Commission on Mental Health. (July 22, 2003). President's New Freedom Commission Report on Mental Health. Retrieved November 12, 2005 from www.mentalhealthcommission.gov/reports/FinalReport/downloads/FinalReport.pdf.

Presly, A.S., Grubb, A.B., & Semple, D. (1982). Predictors of successful rehabilitation in long-stay patients. *Acta Psychiatrica Scandinavica, 65,* 83–88.

Prouteau, A., Verdoux, H., Briand, C., Lesage, A., Lalonde, P., Nicole, L., et al. E. (2004). Self-assessed cognitive dysfunction and objective performance in outpatients with schizophrenia participating in a rehabilitation program. *Schizophrenia Research, 69,* 85–91.

Read, J., & Argyle, N. (1999). Hallucinations, delusions, and thought disorder among adult psychiatric inpatients with a history of child abuse. *Psychiatric Services, 50,* 1467–72.

Read, J., Perry, B.D., Moskowitz, A., & Connolly, J. (2001). The contribution of early traumatic events to schizophrenia in some patients: a traumagenic neurodevelopmental model. *Psychiatry, 64,* 319–345.

Read, J., van Os, J., Morrison, A., & Ross, C. (2005). Childhood trauma, psychosis and schizophrenia: A literature review and clinical implications. *Acta Psychiatrica Scandinavica, 112,* 330–350.

Rector, N.A., & Beck, A.T. (2001). Cognitive behavioral therapy for schizophrenia: An empirical review. *Journal of Nervous and Mental Disease, 189,* 278–87.

Reeder, C., Newton, E., Frangou, S., & Wykes, T. (2004). Which executive skills should we target to affect social functioning and symptom change? A study of a cognitive remediation therapy program. *Schizophrenia Bulletin, 30,* 87–100.

Rifkin, A., Quitkin, F., Kane, J., Klein, D.F., & Ross, D. (1979). The effect of fluphenazine upon social and vocational functioning in remitted schizophrenics. *Biological Psychiatry, 14,* 499–508.

Roe, D. (2001). Progressing from patienthood to personhood across the multidimensional outcomes in schizophrenia and related disorders. *Journal of Nervous and Mental Disease, 189,* 691–699.

Roe, D. (2003). A prospective study on the relationship between self-esteem and functioning during the first year after being hospitalized for psychosis. *Journal of Nervous and Mental Disease, 191,* 45–49.

Rosner, R.I., Lyddon, W.J., & Freeman, A. (2004). Cognitive therapy and dreams: An introduction. In R.I. Rosner, W.J. Lyddon, & A. Freeman (Eds.), *Cognitive therapy and dreams* (pp. 3–8). New York: Springer Publishing Company.

Rupp, A., & Keith, S.J. (1993). The costs of schizophrenia: Assessing the burden. *Psychiatric Clinics of North America, 16,* 413–423.

Sartorius, N., Jablensky, A, & Shapiro, R. (1977). Two-year follow-up of the patients included in the WHO International Pilot Study of Schizophrenia. *Psychological Medicine, 7,* 529–541.

Sanderson, T.L., Best, J.J.K., Doody, G.A., Cunningham Owens, D.G., & Johnstone, E.C. (1999). Neuroanatomy of comorbid schizophrenia and learning disability: A controlled study. *The Lancet, 354,* 1867–1871.

Sass, L.A. (1992). *Madness and modernism.* Cambridge, MA: Harvard University Press.

Sass, L.A., & Parnas, J. (2003). Schizophrenia, consciousness, and the self. *Schizophrenia Bulletin, 29,* 427–444.

Saunders, S.M., & Lueger, R.J. (2005). Evaluation of psychotherapy. In B.J. Sadock & V.A. Sadock (Eds.), *Kaplan & Sadock's comprehensive textbook of psychiatry* (8th Ed.) (pp. 2662–2669). New York: Lippincott, Williams, & Wilkins.

Schenkel, L.S., Spaulding, W.D., DiLillo, D., & Silverstein, S.M. (2005). Histories of childhood maltreatment in schizophrenia: Relationships with premorbid functioning, symptomatology, and cognitive deficits. *Schizophrenia Research, 76,* 273–286.

Schretlen, D., Jayaram, G., Maki, P., Park, K., Abebe, S., & DiCarlo. M. (2000). Demographic, clinical, and neurocognitive correlates of everyday functional impairment in severe mental illness. *Journal of Abnormal Psychology, 109,* 134–138.

Shaner, A., Eckman, T., Roberts, L.J., & Fuller, T. (2003). Feasibility of a skills training approach to reduce substance dependence among individuals with schizophrenia. *Psychiatric Services, 54,* 1287–1289.

Shaw, J.A. (2000). Narcissism as a motivational structure: The problem of personal significance. *Psychiatry, 63,* 219–230.

Siddle, R., & Kingdon, D. (2000). The management of schizophrenia: Cognitive behavioural therapy. *British Journal of Community Nursing, 5,* 20–25.

Silverstein, S.M. (1988). A study of religious conversion in North America. *Genetic, Social, and General Psychology Monographs, 114,* 261–305.

Silverstein, S.M. (1997). Information processing, social cognition, and psychiatric rehabilitation of schizophrenia. *Psychiatry, 60,* 327–340.

Silverstein, S.M. (2000). Psychiatric Rehabilitation of Schizophrenia: Unresolved issues, current trends and future Directions. *Applied and Preventive Psychology, 9,* 227–248.

Silverstein, S.M. (in press). Integration of Jungian and self-psychological perspectives within cognitive behavior therapy for a young man with a fixed religious delusion. *Clinical Case Studies.*

Silverstein, S.M., Bakshi, S., Chapman, R.M., & Nowlis, G. (1998a). Perceptual organisation of configural and nonconfigural visual stimuli in schizophrenia: Effects of repeated exposure. *Cognitive Neuropsychiatry, 3,* 209–223.

Silverstein, S.M., Hatashita-Wong, M., Solak, B.A., Uhlhaas, P., Landa, Y., Wilkniss, S.M., et al. (2005a). Effectiveness of a two-phase cognitive rehabilitation intervention for severely impaired schizophrenia patients. *Psychological Medicine, 35,* 829–837.

Silverstein, S.M., Hitzel, H., & Schenkel, L. (1998c). Cognitive barriers to rehabilitation readiness: Strategies for identification and intervention. *Psychiatric Services, 49,* 34–36.

Silverstein, S.M., Kovács, I., Corry, R., & Valone, C. (2000). Perceptual organization, the disorganization syndrome, and context processing in chronic schizophrenia. *Schizophrenia Research, 43,* 11–20.

Silverstein, S.M., Light, G.A., & Palumbo, D.R. (1998e). The Sustained AttentionTest: A measure of cognitive dysfunction. *Computers in Human Behavior, 14,* 463–475.

Silverstein, S.M., Matteson, S., & Knight, R.A. (1996). Reduced top-down influence in auditory perceptual organization in schizophrenia. *Journal of Abnormal Psychology, 105,* 663–667.

Silverstein, S.M., Menditto, A., & Stuve, P. (2001). Shaping attention span: An operant condition procedure for improving neurocognitive functioning in schizophrenia. *Schizophrenia Bulletin, 27,* 247–257.

Silverstein, S.M., Osborn, L.M., & Palumbo, D.R. (1998d). Rey-Osterreith Complex Figure Test performance in acute, chronic, and outpatient schizophrenia patients. *Journal of Clinical Psychology, 54,* 985–994.

Silverstein, S.M., & Palumbo, D.R. (1995). Nonverbal perceptual organization output disability and schizophrenia spectrum symptomatology. *Psychiatry, 58,* 66–81.

Silverstein, S.M., Pierce, D.L., Saytes, M., Hems, L., Schenkel, L., & Streaker, N. (1998b). Behavioral treatment of attentional dysfunction in chronic, treatment-refractory schizophrenia. *Psychiatric Quarterly, 69,* 95–105.

Silverstein, S.M., Stuve, P., & Menditto, A.A. (1999). Shaping procedures as cognitive retraining techniques in individuals with severe and persistent mental illness. *Psychiatric Rehabilitation Skills, 3,* 59–76.

Silverstein, S.M., Valone, C., Jewell, T.C., Corry, R., Nghiêm, K., Saytes, M., & Potrude, S. (1999). Integrating shaping and skills training techniques in the treatment of chronic, treatment-refractory individuals with schizophrenia. *Psychiatric Rehabilitation Skills, 3,* 41–58.

Silverstein, S.M., Wallace, C.J., & Schenkel, L.S. (2005b). The Micro-Module Learning Tests: Work sample assessments of responsiveness to skills training interventions. *Schizophrenia Bulletin, 31,* 73–83.

Silverstein, S.M., & Wilkniss, S.M. (2004). The future of cognitive rehabilitation of schizophrenia. *Schizophrenia Bulletin, 30,* 679–692.

Simmers, A.J., & Bex, P.J. (2001). Deficit of visual contour integration in dyslexia. *Investigative Ophthalmology and Visual Science, 42,* 2737–2742.

Smith, G.R., Manderscheid, R.W., Flynn, L.M., & Steinwachs, D.M. (1997). Principles for assessment of patient outcomes in mental health care. *Psychiatric Services, 48,* 1033–1036.

Smith, T.E., Hull, J.W., MacKain, S.J., Wallace, C.J., Rattenni, L.A., Goodman, M., Anthony, D.T., & Kentros, M.K. (1996). Training hospitalized patients with schizophrenia in community reintegration skills. *Psychiatric Services, 47,* 1099–1103.

Spaulding, W.D., Fleming, S.K., Reed, D., Sullivan, M., Storzbach, D., & Lam, M. (1999a). Cognitive functioning in schizophrenia: Implications for psychiatric rehabilitation. *Schizophrenia Bulletin, 25,* 275–289.

Spaulding, W.D., Reed, D., Sullivan, M., Richardson, C., & Weiler, M. (1999b). Effects of cognitive treatment in psychiatric rehabilitation. *Schizophrenia Bulletin, 25,* 657–676

Spaulding, W.D., Storms, L., Goodrich, V., & Sullivan, M. (1986). Applications of experimental psychopathology in psychiatric rehabilitation. *Schizophrenia Bulletin, 12,* 560–577.

Spaulding, W., Sullivan, M., & Poland, J. (2003) *Treatment and rehabilitation of severe mental illness.* New York: Guilford.

Stein, L.I., & Test, M.A. (1980). An alternative to mental health treatment. I: Conceptual model, treatment program, and clinical evaluation. *Archives of General Psychiatry, 37,* 392–397.

Stip, E., Caron, J., Renaud, S., Pampoulova, T., & Lecomte, Y. (2003). Exploring cognitive complaints in schizophrenia: the subjective scale to investigate cognition in schizophrenia. *Comprehensive Psychiatry, 44,* 331–340.

Stratta, P., Mancini, F., Mattei, M., Casachia, M., & Rossi, A. (1994). Information processing strategy to remediate Wisconsin Card Sorting Test performance in schizophrenia: A pilot study. *American Journal of Psychiatry, 151,* 915–918.

Strauss, J., & Carpenter, W. (1977). The treatment of acute schizophrenia without drugs: An investigation of some current assumptions. *American Journal of Psychiatry, 134,* 14–20.

Stuve, P.R., & Menditto, A.A. (1999). State hospitals in the new millennium: Rehabilitating the "not ready for rehab players." In H.R. Lamb (Series Ed.) & W. Spaulding (Vol. Ed.), *New directions for mental health services: No. 84. The state hospital in the 21st century* (pp. 35–46). San Francisco: Jossey-Bass Publishers.

Substance Abuse and Mental Health Services Administration (SAMHSA). (2004) Evidence-Based Practices: Shaping Mental Health Services Toward Recovery. Available at http://mentalhealth.samhsa.gov/cmhs/communitysupport/toolkits.

Summerfelt, A.T., Alphs, L.D., Wagman, A.M.I., Funderburk, F.R., Hierholzer, R.M., & Strauss, M.E. (1991a). Reduction of perseverative errors in patients with schizophrenia using monetary feedback. *Journal of Abnormal Psychology, 100,* 613–616.

Summerfelt, A.T., Alphs, L.D., Funderburk, F.R., Strauss, M.E., & Wagman, A.M. (1991b). Impaired Wisconsin Card Sort performance in schizophrenia may reflect motivation deficits (letter). *American Journal of Psychiatry, 151,* 915–918.

Temple, S., & Ho, B.C. (2005). Cognitive therapy for persistent psychosis in schizophrenia: a case-controlled clinical trial. *Schizophrenia Research, 74,* 195–199.

Test, M.A., & Stein, L.I. (1976). Practical guidelines for the community treatment of markedly impaired patients. *Community Mental Health Journal, 12,* 72–82.

Tibbo, P., & Warneke, L. (1999). Obsessive-compulsive disorder in schizophrenia: Epidemiologic and biologic overlap. *Journal of Psychiatry and Neuroscience, 24,* 15–24.

Tienari, P., Wynne, L.C., Sorri, A., Lahti, I., Laksy, K., Moring, J., Naarala, M., Nieminen, P., & Wahlberg, K.E. (2004). Genotype-environment interaction in schizophrenia-spectrum disorder. Long-term follow-up study of Finnish adoptees. *British Journal of Psychiatry. 184,* 216–22.

Tsuang, M.T., Woolson, R.F., & Fleming, J.A. (1979). Long-term outcome of major psychoses. I. Schizophrenia and affective disorders compared with psychiatrically symptom-free surgical conditions. *Archives of General Psychiatry, 36,* 1295–1301.

Uhlhaas, P.J., & Silverstein, S.M. (2005). Perceptual organization in schizophrenia spectrum disorders: Empirical research and theoretical implications. *Psychological Bulletin, 131,* 618–632.

van Der Gaag, M. (1992). *The results of cognitive training in schizophrenic patients.* Delft, The Netherlands: Eburon Publishers.

van Os, J., Castle, D.J., Takei, N., Der G., & Murray, R.M. (1996). Psychotic illness in ethnic minorities: clarification from the 1991 census. *Psychological Medicine, 26,* 203–208.

Velligan, D.I., & Bow-Thomas, C.C. (2000). Two case studies of cognitive adaptation training for outpatients with schizophrenia. *Psychiatric Services, 51,* 25–29.

Velligan, D.I., Lam, F., Ereshefsky, L., & Miller, A.L. (2003). Psychopharmacology: Perspectives on medication adherence and atypical antipsychotic medications. *Psychiatric Services, 54,* 665–667

Velligan, D.I., Prihoda, T.J., Ritch, J.L., Maples, N., Bow-Thomas, C.C., & Dassori, A. (2002). A randomized single-blind pilot study of compensatory strategies in schizophrenia outpatients. *Schizophrenia Bulletin, 28,* 283–292.

Ventura, J., Lukoff, D., Nuechterlein, K.H., Green, M.F., & Shaner, A. (1993). Manual for the Expanded Brief Psychiatric Rating Scale. *International Journal of Methods In Psychiatric Research, 3,* 221–224.

Vidyasagar, T.R. (2001). From attentional gating in macaque primary visual cortex to dyslexia in humans. *Progress in Brain Research, 134,* 297–312.

Vollema, M., Guertsen, G., & Van Voorst, A. (1995). Durable improvements in Wisconsin Card Sort Test performance in schizophrenic patients. *Schizophrenia Research, 16,* 209–215.

Walker, E.F. (1994). Developmentally moderated expressions of the neuropathology underlying schizophrenia. *Schizophrenia Bulletin, 20,* 453–80.

Walker, E.F., & Diforio, D. (1997). Schizophrenia: A neural diathesis-stress model. *Psychological Review, 104,* 667–685.

Wallace, C.J., Lecomte, T.B., Wilde, M.S., & Liberman, R.P. (2001). A consumer-centered assessment for planning individualized treatment and evaluating program outcomes. *Schizophrenia Research, 66,* 59–70.

Wallace, C.J., & Liberman, R.P. (1985). Social skills training for patients with schizophrenia: A controlled clinical trial. *Psychiatry Research, 15,* 239–247.

Wallace, C.J., Liberman, R.P., Kopelowicz, A., & Yaeger, D. (2000). Psychiatric rehabilitation. In N. Andreasen & G.O. Gabbard (Eds.), *Treatment of psychiatric disorders: The DSM-IV edition.* Washington, DC: American Psychiatric Press.

Wallace, C.J., Liberman, R.P., MacKain, S.J., Blackwell, G., & Eckman, T.A. (1992). Effectiveness and replicability of modules for teaching social and instrumental skills to the severely mentally ill. *American Journal of Psychiatry, 149,* 654–658.

Wallace, C.J., & Tauber, R. (2004). Supplementing supported employment with workplace skills training. *Psychiatric Services, 55,* 513–515.

Wallace, C.J., Tauber, R., & Wilde, J. (1999). Teaching fundamental workplace skills to persons with serious mental illness. *Psychiatric Services, 50,* 1147–1149, 1153.

Wexler, B.E., & Bell, M.D. (2005). Cognitive remediation and vocational rehabilitation for schizophrenia. *Schizophrenia Bulletin, 31,* 931–941.

Wexler, B., Hawkins, K., Rounsaville, B., Anderson, M., Sernyak, M., & Green, M. (1997). Normal cognitive performance after extended practice in patients with schizophrenia. *Schizophrenia Research, 26,* 173–180.

Whitehorn, D., Richard, J.C., & Kopala, L.C. (2004). Hospitalization in the first year of treatment for schizophrenia. *Canadian Journal of Psychiatry, 49,* 635–638.

Wilkniss, S.M., Hunter, R.H., & Silverstein, S.M.. (2004). Traitement multimodal de l'agressivité et de la violence chez des personnes souffrant de psychose [Multimodal treatment of aggression and violence in individuals with psychosis]. *Santé Mentale au Quebec, 29,* 143–174.

Williams, L.M., Grieve, S.M., Whitford, T.J., Clark, C.R., Gur, R.C., Goldberg, E., & Flor-Henry, P. (2005). Neural synchrony and gray matter variation in human males and females: An integration of 40 Hz gamma synchrony and MRI measures. *Journal of Integrative Neuroscience,* 77–93.

Wilson, B.A. (1997). Cognitive rehabilitation: How it is and how it might be. *Journal of the International Neuropsychological Society, 3,* 487–496.

Wolwer, W., Frommann, N., Halfmann, S., Piaszek, A., Streit, M., & Gaebel, W. (2005). Remediation of impairments in facial affect recognition in schizophrenia: Efficacy and specificity of a new training program. *Schizophrenia Research, 80,* 295–303.

World Health Organization. (1992). *The ICD-10 Classification of Mental and Behavioural Disorders.* Geneva: Author.

Wu, E.Q., Birnbaum, H.G., Shi, L., Ball, D.E., Kessler, R.C., Moulis, M., & Aggarwal, J. (2005). The economic burden of schizophrenia in the United States in 2002. *Journal of Clinical Psychiatry, 66,* 1122–1129.

Wykes, T., Reeder, C., Corner, J., Williams, C., & Everitt, B. (1999). The effects of neurocognitive remediation on executive processing in patients with schizophrenia. *Schizophrenia Bulletin, 25,* 291–307.

Wykes, T., Reeder, C., Williams, C., Corner, J., Rice, C., & Everitt, B. (2003). Are the effects of cognitive remediation therapy (CRT) durable? Results from an exploratory trial in schizophrenia. *Schizophrenia Research, 61,* 163–174.

Ylvisaker, M., Jacobs, H.E., & Feeney, T. (2003). Positive supports for people who experience behavioral and cognitive disability after brain injury: A review. *Journal of Head Trauma Rehabilitation, 18,* 7–32.

Yolken, R.H., Bachmann, S., Rouslanova, I., Lillehoj, E., Ford, G., Torrey, E.F., & Schroeder, J. (2001). Antibodies to *Toxoplasmosis gondii* in individuals with first-episode schizophrenia. *Clinical Infectious Disease, 32,* 842–844.

Young, J.L., Spitz, R.T., Hillbrand, M., & Daneri, G. (1999). Medication adherence failure in schizophrenia: a forensic review of rates, reasons, treatments, and prospects. *Journal of the American Academy of Psychiatry and The Law, 27,* 426–444.

Zygmunt, A., Olfson, M., Boyer, C.A., & Mechanic, D. (2002). Interventions to improve medication adherence in schizophrenia. *American Journal of Psychiatry, 159,* 1653–1664.

Appendix: Tools and Resources

1. Training: Grid Outlining Best Practices for Recovery and Improved Outcomes for People with Serious Mental Illness

The Training Grid Outlining Best Practices for Recovery and Improved Outcomes for People with Serious Mental Illness was developed by the American Psychological Association's Task Force on Serious Mental Illness. This document should assist providers in identifying appropriate interventions for their settings and those they serve, identifying needed advanced clinical training initiatives, and obtaining access to those clinicians and researchers who have developed, implemented, and/or studied the outcomes of the interventions and instruments described. The most recent version can be accessed at http://www.apa.org/practice/grid.html.

2. Substance Abuse and Mental Health Services Administration (SAMHSA) (2004) Evidence-Based Practices: Shaping Mental Health Services Toward Recovery

Available at http://mentalhealth.samhsa.gov/cmhs/communitysupport/toolkits. This document is part of the large site of the Substance Abuse and Mental Health Services Administration, which can be accessed at www.mentalhealth.samhsa.gov.

3. Schizophrenia.com

Schizophrenia.com is a nonprofit web community providing in-depth information, support and education related to schizophrenia. The website offers a wealth of information and links to additional resources.

4. Alaska Mental Health Consumer Web

Available at http://akmhcweb.org/recovery/rec.htm

5. Boston University, Center for Psychiatric Rehabilitation

Available at www.bu.edu/cpr/recovery

6. Hamilton County Mental Health Board, Cincinnati, Ohio

Available at www.mhrecovery.com

7. The Village Integrated Service Agency, Mental Health Association in Los Angeles County

Available at www.village-isa.org

8. National Recovery and Training Center (NRTC) on Psychiatric Disability, University of Illinois at Chicago. Self Determination Project

Available at www.psych.uic.edu/uicnrtc

9. National Alliance for the Mentally Ill (NAMI)

Available at www.nami.org

10. NAMI of Santa Cruz County, CA

Available at www.namiscc.org/Recovery

11. National Institute of Mental Health

Available at www.nimh.nih.gov

12. National Mental Health Association

Available at www.nmha.org

13. U.S. Department of Health and Human Services

Available at www.hhs.gov

14. Adult Recovery Network

Available at http://adultrecoverynetwork.org/content/celrecovery/ORB_Spreads _v2.pdf. This website contains a helpful booklet on recovery from serious mental illness. The booklet has listings of books, articles, and websites that can provide further information.

15. Heuristic Model

From Nuechterlein, K.H., Dawson, M.E., Gitlin, M., Ventura, J., Goldstein, M.J., Snyder, K.S., Yee, C.M., & Mintz, J. (1992). Developmental processes in schizophrenic disorders: Longitudinal studies of vulnerability and stress. *Schizophrenia Bulletin, 18,* 387–425. Reprinted by permission. (See the following page.)

A tentative heuristic framework for some of the possible psychobiological vulnerability factors, nonspecific environmental stressors, and protective factors in schizophrenic relapse and illness course

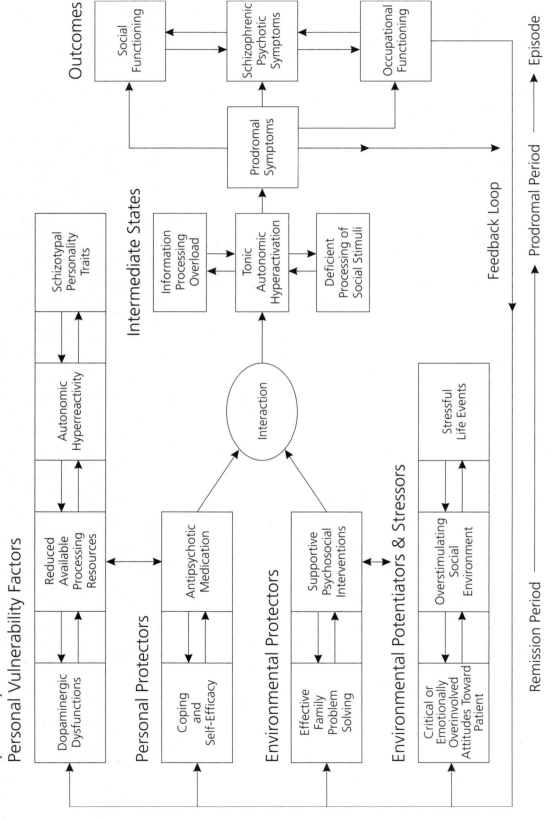

Obsessive-Compulsive Disorder

In the series: Advances in Psychotherapy – Evidence-Based Practice, Volume 3

Jonathan S. Abramowitz

Based on decades of scientific research and clinical refinement, cognitive-behavioral therapy using the techniques of exposure and response prevention has helped countless individuals with OCD overcome debilitating symptoms and live fuller, more satisfying lives. From leading expert Jonathan S. Abramowitz, this volume opens with an overview of the diagnosis and assessment of OCD and delineates a research-based conceptual framework for understanding the development, maintenance, and treatment of obsessions and compulsions. The core of the book is a highly practical treatment manual packed with helpful clinical pearls, therapist-patient dialogs, illustrative case vignettes, and sample forms and handouts. Readers are equipped with skills for tailoring exposure and response prevention techniques for patients with different types of OCD symptoms, including washing, checking, ordering, obsessions, and mental rituals. The book, which also addresses common obstacles in treating individuals with OCD, represents an essential resource for anyone providing services for individuals

Jonathan S. Abramowitz

Obsessive-Compulsive Disorder

Advances in Psychotherapy
Evidence-Based Practice

HOGREFE

2006, 104 pages, softcover
ISBN: 0-88937-316-7 , US $ / € 24.95
Standing order price US $ / € 19.95
(minimum 4 successive vols.)
*Special rates for members of the Society of Clinical Psychology (APA D12) - Single volume: US $19.95
- Standing order: US $17.95 per volume
(please supply APA membership # when ordering)

> *"Dr. Abramowitz has done a remarkable job in taking difficult to understand concepts and making them easy to grasp. This is the most practical, user-friendly guide to date. It is a quick, but informative read by one of the premier thought leaders in the field of OCD. This is a must read for clinicians and students alike, and will be required reading for our staff and trainees."*
> Bradley C. Riemann, PhD, Clinical Director, OCD Center at Rogers Memorial Hospital, Oconomowoc, WI

Essential reading for anyone treating patients with OCD.

Table of Contents

Order online at: **www.hhpub.com**

HOGREFE

Childhood Maltreatment

In the series: Advances in Psychotherapy – Evidence-Based Practice, Volume 4

Christine Wekerle, Alec L. Miller, David A. Wolfe, Carrie B. Spindel

The serious consequences of child abuse or maltreatment are among the most challenging things therapists encounter. In recent years there has been a surge of interest, and of both basic and clinical research, concerning early traumatization. This volume in the series *Advances in Psychotherapy* integrates results from the latest research showing the importance of early traumatization into a compact and practical guide for practitioners. Advances in biological knowledge have highlighted the potential chronicity of effects of childhood maltreatment, demonstrating particular life challenges in managing emotions, forming and maintaining healthy relationships, healthy coping, and holding a positive outlook of oneself. Despite the resiliency of many maltreated children, adolescent and young adult well-being is often compromised. This text first overviews our current knowledge of the effects of childhood maltreatment on psychiatric and psychological health, then provides diagnostic guidance, and subsequently goes on to profile promising and effective evidence-based interventions. Consistent with the discussions of treatment, prevention programming that is multi-targeted at issues for maltreated individuals is highlighted. This text helps the practitioner or student to know what to look for, what questions need to be asked, how to handle the sensitive ethical implications, and what are promising avenues for effective coping.

Christine Wekerle · Alec L. Miller · David A. Wolfe · Carrie B. Spindel

Childhood Maltreatment

Advances in Psychotherapy
Evidence-Based Practice

HOGREFE

2006, 98 pages, softcover
ISBN: 0-88937-314-0, US $ / € 24.95
Standing order price US $ / € 19.95
(minimum 4 successive vols.)
*Special rates for members of the Society of Clinical Psychology (APA D12) - Single volume: US $19.95
· Standing order: US $17.95 per volume
(please supply APA membership # when ordering)

Compact guidance for practitioners dealing with one of the greatest challenges in clinical practice.

Table of Contents
Dedication • Acknowledgments
1. Description • Terminology • Definition • Epidemiology • Course and Prognosis
2. Theories and Models of the Effects of Childhood Maltreatment • PTSD Symptomatology Model • Social Cognitive Information Processing Models
3. Diagnosis and Treatment Indications • Psychiatric Impairment and Specific Disorders Associated with Childhood Maltreatment
4. Treatment: Intervening with Childhood Maltreatment Victims • Methods of Treatment • Mechanisms of Action: Components of Trauma-Focused Cognitive Behavioral Treatment • Efficacy and Prognosis • Variations and Combinations of Methods • Problems and Issues in Carrying Out the Treatments
5. Case Vignette • 6. Further Reading • 7. References • 8. Appendix: Tools and Resources

Order online at: **www.hhpub.com**

HOGREFE

Advances in Psychotherapy – Evidence-Based Practice

Developed and edited in consultation with the Society of Clinical Psychology (APA Division 12).

Pricing / Standing Order Terms

Regular Prices: Single-volume – $24.95; Series Standing Order – $19.95
APA D12 member prices: Single-volume – $19.95; Series Standing Order – $17.95
With a Series Standing Order you will automatically be sent each new volume upon its release. After a minimum of 4 successive volumes, the Series Standing Order can be cancelled at any time. If you wish to pay by credit card, we will hold the details on file but your card will only be charged when a new volume actually ships.

Order Form (please check a box)

[ ]	I would like to place a Standing Order for the series at the special price of US $ / €19.95 per volume, starting with volume no. ....
[ ]	I am a D12 Member and would like to place a Standing Order for the series at the special D12 Member Price of US $ / € 17.95 per volume, starting with volume no. ...... My APA D12 membership no. is:
[ ]	I would like to order the following single volumes at the regular price of US $ / € 24.95 per volume.
[ ]	I am a D12 Member and would like to order the following single volumes at the special D12 Member Price of US $ / € 19.95 per volume. My APA D12 membership no. is:

Qty.	Author / Title / ISBN	Price	Total
		Subtotal	
	WA residents add 8.8% sales tax; Canadians 7% GST		
	Shipping & handling: USA – US $6.00 per volume (multiple copies: US $1.25 for each further copy) Canada – US $8.00 per volume (multiple copies: US $2.00 for each further copy) South America: – US $10.00 per volume (multiple copies: US $2.00 for each further copy) Europe: – € 6.00 per volume (multiple copies: € 1.25 for each further copy) Rest of the World: – € 8.00 per volume (multiple copies: € 1.50 for each further copy)		
		Total	

[ ] Check enclosed　　　　[ ] Please bill me　　　　[ ] Charge my:　[ ] VISA　　[ ] MC　　[ ] AmEx

Card # _____ CVV2/CVC2/CID # _____ Exp date _____

Signature _____

Shipping address (please include phone & fax) _____

_____

_____

_____

Order online at: **www.hhpub.com**

Hogrefe & Huber Publishers · 30 Amberwood Parkway · Ashland, OH 44805 · Tel: (800) 228-3749 · Fax: (419) 281-6883
Hogrefe & Huber Publishers · Rohnsweg 25 · D-37085 Göttingen, Germany · Tel: +49 551 49609-0 · Fax: +49 551 49609-88
E-Mail: custserv@hogrefe.com

HOGREFE